Death is the mother of beauty

Death is the mother of beauty

MIND, METAPHOR, CRITICISM

Mark Turner

The University of Chicago Press
Chicago and London

MARK TURNER is assistant professor of English,
University of Chicago.

The University of Chicago Press, Chicago 60637
The University of Chicago Press, Ltd., London

96 95 94 93 92 91 90 89 88 87   5 4 3 2 1

Library of Congress Cataloguing-in-Publication Data

Turner, Mark, 1954–
    Death is the mother of beauty.

    Bibliography: p.
    Includes index.
    1. Metaphor. 2. Kinship—Terminology.
3. Semantics. 4. Causation. 5. English poetry—
History and criticism. I. Title.
    PN228.M4T87 1987   821'.009   87-5998
    ISBN 0-226-81721-0
    ISBN 0-226-81722-9 (pbk.)

88-B77

Contents

Foreword

by George Lakoff

This is a truly interdisciplinary book, a book of importance both to literary scholars and to scientists of the mind—linguists, psychologists, anthropologists, and researchers in artificial intelligence. It shows that the study of the literary mind is an integral part of the study of the mind in general. And it shows clearly that everyday language and literary language are not separate domains, that discoveries about one bear on the other. Beyond being a book about literature, it is a book about semantics, about the representation of knowledge, about cultural description, and about important philosophical concepts such as causation and similarity.

Turner takes as his laboratory for conceptual analysis the entire range of the metaphorical uses of kinship expressions in the body of high-canon poetry in English from Chaucer to Wallace Stevens. This includes thousands of examples that, on the surface, seem widely disparate. He masterfully shows how this enormous range of examples can be accounted for by a handful of general conceptual metaphors which give rise to ten inference patterns through their interactions with our folk theories, both about kinship and other matters. What is particularly impressive about the analysis is his focus on inference—on how we reason using these metaphors. What Turner explains is why these metaphors mean what they mean—including their connotations.

Why is this work of interest to a metaphor scholar? Because traditional theories of metaphor assume that metaphors occur one by one, that each distinct metaphorical expression is individually created. Moreover, it is traditionally assumed that metaphor is a matter of language and not of conceptual structure. In showing that thousands of distinct metaphorical expressions reduce to a handful of conceptual metaphorical structures, Turner disproves both traditional views.

Why is this work of interest to a linguist? There is a long history in linguistics of using kinship terms as a model for semantic analysis, as a showcase illustration of one's favorite theory. For instance, in theories that use semantic features (See Katz and Fodor, 1964), *mother* is represented in terms of a componential analysis in which there is a conjunction of two primitive features: FEMALE and PARENT. In theories that use meaning postulates to define concepts, such an analysis takes the form of MOTHER(X,Y) → FEMALE(X) AND PARENT(X,Y). Such analyses come out of a linguistic tradition of providing semantic analyses that make *minimal distinctions* among terms in the same semantic fields. If one wants to minimally distinguish *mother* from *father*, this is how to do it.

What Turner shows is that such analyses are ludicrously simpleminded, and he does so on the basis of what is ordinarily taken to be the main task of semantics: accounting for patterns of inference and for how expressions are understood. Turner shows that, in order to account for the ways in which kinship terms in literary texts are understood, what is required is an elaborate description of our everyday folk theory of kinship, plus a collection of basic conceptual metaphors and metonymies. He also shows that literary texts make use of complex patterns of metaphorical reasoning, which should not even exist if classical semantic theories are correct. Turner's analysis thus gives the lie to the idea that literary metaphor is ornamental rather than inferential in nature. Since semantics concerns inference, Turner's work shows that metaphor is central, not peripheral, to the concerns of semantics. Adequate linguistic analyses in the domain of semantics must therefore include all the apparatus that Turner shows to be necessary to account for inference: folk theories, conceptual metaphors, and metonymies.

Why is this book of interest to philosophers? Philosophers are concerned, among other things, with understanding very basic human concepts, among them, causation. Turner's chapter 4 takes up the nature of causation in great detail. He argues that the approaches to causation that philosophers have taken have been inadequate for a wide range of examples. He then goes on to argue persuasively that such cases of causation are actually understood metaphorically in terms of the conceptual kinship metaphors he has investigated, even when no actual kinship expression is present. His main contribution in this chapter is to provide an account of how we understand mental causation. He argues that mental causation is understood as progeneration, in terms of the entire complex of gestation, birth, nurturance, etc.

Why is this book of interest to anthropologists? No field has traditionally been more concerned with the subject matter of kinship than anthropology. Anthropologists have seen more clearly than other scholars the central role that kinship plays in culture. Turner's work adds an additional dimension to our understanding of how pervasive the influence of kinship is in culture. He demonstrates how kinship concepts are not merely about kinship, but extend metaphorically to other domains: causation, similarity, even the very concept of taxonomic categorization.

Why is this book of interest to researchers in artificial intelligence? The study of analogical reasoning has become one of the principal fields of study in AI research. AI researchers have realized that people do reason on the basis of analogy and have proposed theories of various kinds to account for the phenomenon: theories of feature-changing, structure-mapping, and shared axiom structures. Turner's elaborate analysis of kinship metaphor has all the properties of a complex system of analogical reasoning. In fact, it is one of the most extensive and complex systems analyzed to date. Turner's analysis suggests that all of the current theories are flawed in one way or another, and his technique of analysis suggests how some of those flaws might be rectified.

Turner is a unique figure, both a literary scholar and a cognitive scientist. In an earlier day, such a combination of talents would have been the norm. There was a time when it would have been unthinkable for scholars studying the various aspects of the mind *not* to have a thorough knowledge of literature and to use that knowledge. Correspondingly, there was a time when being a literary scholar entailed finding out all that one could about the nature of mind and bringing that knowledge to bear on what one wrote. This book shows why it is crucial to return to such traditions—how insights derived from the study of literature can contribute significantly to cognitive science, and how an understanding of the mechanisms of mind provides indispensable tools for literary analysis.

Acknowledgments

To Wayne Booth and George Lakoff, for sustained criticism and encouragement, my debt is high. On the same account, thanks go to Julian Boyd, Philip Damon, and Joseph Williams. My two anonymous readers for the University of Chicago Press were unusually intelligent and thorough.

I am grateful to Claudia Brugman, Bettina Nicely, Eve Sweetser, and William Veeder for readings. I have benefited from conversations about parts of this book with Joel Altman, Stephen Greenblatt, Greg Meagher, Jenny Schaffer, William Wimsatt, Seth Katz, and many colleagues and students in the departments of English and linguistics and the Committee on Cognition and Communication at the University of Chicago, and the departments of English and Linguistics and the Institute of Cognitive Studies at the University of California, Berkeley.

I am grateful to the National Endowment for the Humanities for a year's Fellowship for Independent Study and Research, no. FA-26105-86, which helped me finish this book. The Institute of Cognitive Studies, at the University of California, Berkeley, under the acting directorship of Charles J. Fillmore, has been invaluably hospitable.

Death is the mother of beauty

1   *Introduction*

This book is a modern rhetoric which explores issues central to literary theory, cognitive science, and linguistics. Classical rhetoric sought to discover what knowledge and thought members of an audience brought to communication. How could a speaker, through language, move his audience from one locus of thought to another? What were the *common-places* of knowledge? What were the connections between *thought* and *language*, and how could one work those connections to evoke, invent, and persuade? Aristotle wanted to know how *figures of diction* connect with *figures of thought*. Cicero held that rhetoric's beginning, which other parts of rhetoric serve to unfold, is mental *invention* or *conception*. He explored some processes by which we *invent*.

Rhetoric degenerated (as Paul Ricoeur chronicles in chapter 2 of *The Rule of Metaphor*) when it abandoned thought for style. Inattentive to mind underlying surface forms of language, rhetoric reduced itself to cataloguing what it took to be kinds of surface wordplay as if they had no analogues in cognition. Rhetoric thereby lost its ability to tell us anything about thought and language and so became peripheral, until recent rhetorics, such as Wayne Booth's *Rhetoric of Irony* (1974), revived classical rhetoric.

The revival has been aided by contemporary work on the theory of metaphor within linguistics and the cognitive sciences. This work has emphasized that metaphor is not merely a matter of *words* but is rather a fundamental mode of *cognition* affecting all human thought and action, including everyday language and poetic language.*

Here, I want to start to develop a mode of analysis that I take to be the natural successor to classical rhetoric. This mode of analysis begins with the fact that audiences share many things—conceptual systems, social practices, commonplace knowledge, discourse genres, and every aspect of a common language, including syntax, semantics, morphology, and phonology. Rhetoric seeks to analyze all these common cognitive systems of audiences and the ways in which they can be used. The job of rhetoric thus overlaps with the job of the cognitive sciences.

Modern literary criticism does not ordinarily begin from this perspective. It typically begins not by analyzing the cognitive apparatus underlying language but rather by assuming and using that apparatus to conduct conversations that are often extensions of literature. We hold conversations for many reasons: to learn about the world, to discover the opinions of others, to situate ourselves in our communities and traditions, to develop a sense of aesthetics or ethics, and so on. Modern literary critical traditions typically extend such conversations legitimately. Conversations, we all concede, can be interesting even if the conversants do not understand the linguistic and cognitive processes allowing them to converse. Similarly, we all feel that a performance by a dancer can be compelling even if the dancer has not analyzed the biophysics of the human muscular and skeletal systems. Just so, we all grant that a piece of literary criticism might be worthwhile even if the literary critic does not understand the cognitive apparatus underlying language and literature.

But there are dangers and losses that arise from the literary critic's typical beginning point. Literary criticism usually assumes that we understand the cognitive apparatus underlying language and literature, when, in fact, the analysis has only begun. This cognitive apparatus dominantly informs any conversation we may hold and any literature we may write and any criticism we may conduct. It underlies all

*See William Nagy (1974), Michael Reddy (1979), and George Lakoff and Mark Johnson (1980).

literary subtleties. When a literary critic presupposes that he or she understands that apparatus and proceeds to analyze subtleties that derive from it, the literary critic may be *simply mistaken* in the presupposition. This may vitiate the worth of the consequent analysis. Someone who has not studied tonality might analyze a Bach cantata in many beguiling ways, but would be in constant danger of pinning the analysis on mistaken presuppositions about the workings of music. Literary criticism typically finds itself in this dangerous position.

An example is deconstructive criticism. This mode of criticism begins with the view that linguistic meaning is inherently unanchored.* Deconstructive criticism derives this view by uncritically accepting a literary critical extension of a basic concept belonging to Saussurian linguistics. Ferdinand de Saussure correctly observed that phonemes are determined on the basis of distributional contrasts within a phonemic system. For example, the phoneme /t/ at the beginning of "time" contrasts with the phoneme /d/ at the beginning of "dime." It is partially because "time" and "dime" are used as two different words that we know that /t/ and /d/ are phonemic and in contrast. Thus, how an acoustic instance of a phoneme works is not just a matter of its sounds. An acoustic instance of a phoneme also works by virtue of the fact that there are relationships between phonemes. For instance, we know that the phonemes /t/ and /d/ contrast with each other. We know from our language that in certain contexts either /t/ or /d/ can occur, and it can

---

*Many theorists have argued that signs are polymorphous. Charles Sanders Peirce (1931) claimed that a sign is interpreted into a different sign, an *interpretant*, which can be interpreted into another *interpretant*, and so on ad infinitum. Louis Hjelmslev (1969) maintained that after the denotative semiotic of an utterance is processed, the results can be a connotative semiotic that may again be processed. Roland Barthes, in both *S/Z* (1974) and *Mythologies* (1972), has claimed that there is no denotative, no basic, no first meaning prior to the work of connotation. And Jacques Derrida in *Of Grammatology* (1976) has perhaps pushed this furthest in the claim that all meaning is displacement of term by term, that "the signified always already functions as a signifier. . . . There is not a single signified that escapes . . . the play of signifying references that constitute language" (p. 7).

make a difference which one actually occurs in a given instance.

For a more complicated example of relationships between phonemes, take the words "writer" and "rider." Many speakers of English, myself included, pronounce these as [rayDr] and [ra:yDr] respectively. In pronunciation, the distinction between phonemic /t/ and /d/ is neutralized to the phone known as flap-[D] and appears instead in the difference in the length of the vowel, /ay/ versus /a:y/. Thus, in the absence of context we cannot tell whether the sound [D] is an instance of the voiceless phoneme /t/ or the element that it minimally contrasts with, the voiced phoneme /d/. This shows that what makes something phonemic in a language is a matter of complicated relationships within the phonological system of the language.

Saussure's correct observation about phones and phonemes has been incorrectly extended in deconstructionist criticism to lexemes—for the most part, words. The details of this extension have never been anything but murky, but I take it that the details run something like this. Lexemes get their meaning only by virtue of distributional contrasts within the lexemic system of the language. A phoneme or a lexeme, so the logic goes, *consists in* the traces of what it contrasts with. So what is present *consists in* traces of what is absent. A lexeme *consists in* traces of other lexemes that it is not. So everything consists not only in its opposite but also in everything else it is not.

This deconstructionist conclusion derives from two assumptions. First, phonemes consist in traces of what they contrast with. (Saussure, on my reading, never said this, and the notion that the phonemic system is grounded nowhere but in itself has been discredited by modern linguistic research. But let the first assumption pass.) Second, lexemes work like phonemes. This assumption is wrong on a grand scale.

Once these two presuppositions are made, it is easy to make arguments like the following: Just as the sound [D] can be assigned to either of two minimally contrasting phonemes, /t/ and /d/, so any word can be assigned to either a given meaning or its opposite. Further, so the logic seems to go, since a meaning and its opposite are contradictory, a word can have contradictory meanings, and if a word can have contradictory meanings, it can mean anything. Analysis of meaning is replaced by and subsumed by analysis of meaning-contrast. Consider some minimal contrasts in word meaning: *presence-absence*, *up-down*, *mother-father*. To the deconstructive critic, *presence* can mean *absence*, or anything else; *up* can mean *down*, or anything else; *mother* can mean *father*, or anything else. There is, the claim goes, "free play of signifiers," which means that the critic can interpret without limit or constraint and the author can never be in control of his language. This gives ultimate power to critics over authors.

But words are not sound segments and meanings are not phonemes. The putative linguistics presupposed by the principle of the free play of signifiers has no serious basis in contemporary linguistics or cognitive science. If anything, the opposite seems to be true.* Semantics is constrained by our models of ourselves and our worlds. We have models of *up* and *down* that are based on the way our bodies actually function. Once the word "up" is given its meaning relative to our experience with gravity, it is not free to "slip" into its opposite. "Up" means up and not down. Lexemes may use some contrasts. We know that *presence* minimally contrasts with *absence*. But that does not mean that lexemes *consist in* traces of their opposites. On the contrary, semantics mainly *consists in* connections between our language and our cognitive models of ourselves and our worlds. We have a model that men and women couple to produce offspring who are

---

*Meaning is anchored and constrained in various ways. Lakoff (1986) provides a survey of much of the relevant research. For research on the perceptual and motor basis of basic level categorization, see Rosch 1976, 1977, Berlin 1974, Tversky 1985 (and in press). For research on how words and groups of related words are defined relative to frames, see Fillmore 1975, 1976, 1978, 1982a, 1982b, 1985. For research on the biological basis of semantic categorization, see Kay & McDaniel 1978. For research on the role of image structure in semantics, see Talmy 1972, 1975, 1978, 1985, Langacker 1987, Lindner 1981, Brugman 1981, 1983, Casad 1982, Janda 1984. For research on cognitive constraints on historical semantic change, see Sweetser 1987. For research on physical and experiential constraints on metaphor, see Lakoff and Johnson 1980, Johnson (in press).

similar to their parents, and this model is grounded in genetics, and the semantics of kinship metaphor is grounded in this model. Mothers have a different role than fathers in this model, and thus there is a reason why "Death is the father of beauty" fails poetically while "Death is the mother of beauty" succeeds. The meanings of kinship words are not free to commute away from these anchoring basic models and basic processes without some tension, friction, and resistance.

Deconstructive readings rely on the principle of the free play of signifiers, but this principle is mistaken. We may, of course, call into use all sorts of knowledge in our reading of a text and thereby produce supplementary variant readings, but that does not mean that texts are free to *slip* without constraint. On the contrary, though a text may result in various readings, *all* of these readings are constrained by our modes of cognition. So deconstructive criticism, like most literary criticism, is in the dangerous position of pinning its analyses on potentially mistaken presuppositions about thought, knowledge, and language.

My intention is not to change the fundamental job of the literary critic, which is to hold worthwhile conversations about literature, but rather to give him or her the tools to do it responsibly and to do it better. At present, most literary critics do not know what is and is not known about cognition and language. Such awareness is required for a literary critic to gauge the implications of his assertions, to know whether his presuppositions are controversial or safe or plainly mistaken. Everyone agrees that "Death is the mother of beauty" is a magnificent line. Can we explain why it is a better line than "Death is the father of beauty" or "Death is parent of beauty"? Why is "Death is the fraternal twin brother of beauty" a clunker?

To know exactly why "Death is the mother of beauty" is striking and why some other kinship terms will not do in the place of "mother" requires us to understand a great deal. It requires that we understand both the idealized cognitive models of kinship roles in our culture and the metaphors that interact with them to yield metaphoric inferences. That is, it requires precisely the kind of analysis I provide in this book.

The losses that accompany not knowing the connections between thought, knowledge, and language are too great for literary critical traditions to continue to sustain. Good literature is powerful because it masterfully evokes and manipulates our cognitive apparatus. How it does so is of interest to anyone concerned with mind. Modern literary criticism, because it is not concerned with these general cognitive capacities, rarely addresses the source of literature's power. Systematically, by misemphasis, it obscures literature's forceful connections to other kinds of human thought and knowledge. Consequently, modern literary criticism is often regarded as a monadic, isolationary practice.

One of the principal reasons that we study literature is to understand the workings of the human mind. There are certain things about the human mind that we can see best by looking at literature. Writers, as Pound says, are the antennae of the race. Writers constantly explore our conceptual and linguistic structures and push these structures to see how they respond and where they break. What the writer has to teach us cannot be learned except by studying literature, and it is the literary critic, not the cognitive psychologist or linguist, who is trained to study literature. So if the literary critic does not attend to this job, no one else will be able to, and the potential benefits of doing the job will be lost.

The literary critic, certainly since the Romantic Age, has typically been content to let the scientist, including the scientist of mind, go about his investigations, while the critic conducts his readings of specific literary texts, as if the two enterprises were unconnected. This has robbed the science of mind of a major source of insight, and it has likewise robbed literary studies of their influence on the nonliterary world. Who now reads literary criticism besides literary critics?

This is a great loss, and a needless loss. What the literary critic has to teach about the mind is indispensable to the work of linguists, psychologists, philosophers of science, cognitive scientists, philosophers of mind, anthropologists, and any human being who wishes to understand his or her nature. For example, metaphor, to which the literary critic is minutely attuned, is not just a matter of literary wordplay, not even just a matter of language—it is a pattern of thought that underlies our cognition and knowledge generally, including our cognition and knowledge about our daily worlds, about love, about quarks, about family, about nuclear arms, about rape, about mathematics, about gender, about economics, and about the body. When the literary critic speaks about a metaphor, he or she is speaking about principles of thought—manifested in a certain kind of language. Since these principles of thought are fundamental to all other human sciences, the literary critic's claims must place something at stake for all these disciplines.

The literary critic has much to contribute to the analysis of the cognitive apparatus fundamental to literature, but other kinds of researchers, such as linguists, psychologists, and neurobiologists, also have much to contribute, which means that literary critics and these other kinds of researchers should be working together at the enterprise. This should, I think, be the natural outcome of a revised and updated version of classical rhetoric.

Classical rhetoric would have regarded literature as the apt place to begin inquiry into anything concerning the human mind. But now we are in the stultifying position of intelligent people assuming that literature and science, including the science of the mind, have nothing to do with each other. I want to begin to demonstrate how impoverishing this mistake has been.

The rhetorical approach to literary texts that I would like to revive and place in a contemporary context is thus rather different from the dominant approach in literary criticism. When a critic proposes to examine a text, the literary critical profession usually calls down the principles of *canonical texts* and *novelty of reading*, leading to the questions, Does this critic offer a new reading of a canonical text? Does he show us in the text meaning that we have previously missed? Under the rubric of not rehearsing the obvious, the critic ordinarily skips over those places where a text seems straightforward or a reading natural, unless some insight can be introduced that will complicate the straightforwardness or alienate the naturalness. But this critical jump skips the harder and prior question: How can a text ever seem straightforward? A reader's quick understanding of a line like "The day is a woman who loves you" forms, hand in

hand with the author's generating the line, the most dazzling phenomenon the literary critic confronts, and the one
for which literary criticism offers the shallowest explanations,
or none at all. What must the mind of the reader be, that it
can (rather speedily) understand a text, and what must a text
be, that the mind of a reader can understand it? We understand a text by assuming that it invites us to employ techniques we already possess to work on things we already
know. What are the processes and knowledge our linguistic
and literary community expects us to possess?

Such a rhetorical approach places literature and language
back at the center of the investigation of mind. If we wish
to know how people conceive of and model reality, let us
look at their patterns of language and invention. Literature
and cognition are doors into each other: literature leads us to
questions about human understanding, and the study of the
human mind turns wisely for clues to the oldest and most
abiding arts.

To begin to develop a mode of analyzing the connections
between thought, knowledge, language, and literature, I
need a laboratory. This laboratory should involve some fundamental kind of thought (e.g., metaphoric thought), some
fundamental kind of knowledge (e.g., our models of family),
some powerful kind of language (e.g., kinship metaphors,
like "Necessity is the mother of invention") connected with
these kinds of thought and knowledge, and some important
kind of literature (e.g., extended literary kinship metaphors)
connected with all three. I have chosen kinship metaphor as
the laboratory—though others would have served—because
kinship metaphor meets these criteria and is rich in other
ways appropriate to the project. The particular powerful kind
of thought and the particular powerful kind of knowledge
that combine in kinship metaphor are strongly and deeply
interdependent. One way to understand the abstract notion
metaphor is in terms of what we know about *kinship*. Often,
we think of two concepts as bearing a metaphoric relation
because they resemble each other. We may understand the
notions of *relation* and *resemblance* in terms of *kin relation*
and *family resemblance*. So we may understand the abstract
notion *metaphor* by seeing that it stands in metaphoric relation to *kinship*.

This is not surprising when we consider that we often place things into the same category on the basis of what has been called *family resemblance*. Family resemblances are perhaps the similarities that from infancy we notice most. And we use just this concept of similarity to help explain to ourselves how two things can bear a metaphorical relation or resemblance. In short, we explain *metaphor* to ourselves in terms of what we know about *family*.

Kinship metaphor also leads us directly to the study of the human mind along other paths. I will show in the chapter on metaphor and kin that analysis of kinship metaphor reveals a mental model we use to produce and understand certain kinds of language about mind. I will argue in the chapter on causation that kinship metaphor provides the basic metaphors we use to understand *mental creation*. Some other justifications equally strong will emerge as the text unfolds.

In exploring this laboratory of kinship metaphor, I bring together ordinary and literary language. This may seem odd to most linguists and literary critics, since they share a fundamental misconception about language. Most linguists and literary critics share the pernicious assumption that ordinary everyday language and literary language are separate realms to be investigated separately. Linguists and literary critics hold these views for different reasons. The dominant modern tradition in linguistics concerns itself with what it takes to be ordinary literal language. It assumes that literary language is parasitic on ordinary literal language and therefore is of peripheral, rather than central, interest. The dominant modern tradition in literary criticism assumes that ordinary language is simple, well understood, and "common" in the sense of not being sufficiently refined. Since the literary critic is concerned with the refinements of language, he feels comfortable taking ordinary language for granted and studying only literary language. But in fact the processes underlying literary refinements belong to ordinary language, and the refinements themselves derive from and depend on structures of ordinary language. Conversely, processes such as metaphor and metonymy, which most linguists deport to the alien realm of literature, are implicit and indispensable in ordinary language. Moreover, the most common processes of ordinary language frequently appear in their highest relief and most compelling manifestations in literature. So the linguist committed to studying ordinary language must take literature as part of what he seeks to study and explain and will be helped in his chosen task by doing so. And the literary critic who seeks to understand the refined use a particular author makes of language must understand how that author is employing the cognitive apparatus underlying ordinary language.

Two aspects of my methodology call for discussion. First, I usually analyze kinship metaphors decontextualized. In doing so, I do not mean to imply that a textually situated kinship metaphor does not lose aspects of its meaning when lifted from context. Of course it must. But I am interested in the patterns of meaning that run through all these kinship metaphors. These patterns of meaning transcend local textual manifestations because they are part of our cognitive capacity for metaphor and our cognitive models of kinship, derived from our participation in our linguistic and literary communities. Take, for example, "I am a child of the modern age." I am not discussing the special effects of the discursive situation from which this kinship metaphor is drawn. We all understand the metaphor in a certain way when it is removed from discursive context, and it is that understanding alone that I will be dealing with.

Second, I often juxtapose literary texts from various cultures, languages, and epochs within the Western literary tradition. Some structuralists have been justifiably attacked for doing something ostensibly similar, in particular for ignoring wide-ranging cultural and linguistic differences around the world. (See, e.g., Paul Ricoeur's critique of Claude Lévi-Strauss, "Structure and Hermeneutics," in *The Conflict of Interpretations*.) This work differs in taking as its literary domain what counts as a single cultural tradition with respect to kinship metaphor, namely, the Western literary tradition.

Still, there may be confusion about how this book relates to the study of culture because the debate between structuralism and hermeneutics has sometimes led to the fuzzy notion that research into common mental systems somehow inherently slights the role of culture, which is wrong. Artifacts aside, culture is embodied in the mind. It is the major insight of cognitive anthropology that in order to study culture one must study cognition, that is, the conceptual structures employed by the members of that culture. That is one of the things this book seeks to do.

The main thing this book seeks to achieve is a bringing together of certain kinds of researchers typically isolated from each other. It is not apt for some people to work on semantics, others to work on literature, and others to work on the nature of mind without taking into account one another's insights.

2   Metaphor and Kin

2.1 Introduction

Literary language abounds with the metaphorical uses of kinship terms, from the Biblical "Babylon is the mother of harlots and abominations" to Stevens's "The moon is the mother of pathos and pity" to Donne's "Darknesse, lights elder brother" and Sidney's "Invention, nature's child, fled Stepdame Study's blows." They occur in everything from proverbs like "Necessity is the mother of invention" or "A proverb is the child of experience" to popular song lyrics like Randy Newman's "I'm the son of the prairie and the wind that sweeps the plain" or the Jefferson Airplane's "Science is mankind's brother." How can we understand and invent so many so easily?

A handful of basic conceptual metaphors accounts for all of these and for an infinity of expressions beyond them. Each of these expressions is a specific linguistic metaphor, that is, a metaphorical idea expressed in words. But the metaphorical ideas themselves are conceptual matters, matters of thought that underlie the particular words that express them. While there is an infinity of such expressions at the level of particular words, they all derive from a few basic metaphors at the conceptual level; these combine and interact with our knowledge of kinship to yield ten basic metaphoric inference patterns about kinship. All of the reasoning that we do when we invent or understand a kinship metaphor is an application of some combination of these ten patterns of inference.

Imagination is thus not unfettered; it is governed by principles. These principles are automatic and below the level of consciousness. The job here is to show just what some of these principles are. When a literary critic, a linguist, or for that matter anyone at all, interprets a metaphor as meaning such-and-such, he is drawing upon our ability to use these principles, just as a speaker of a language uses principles of syntax and semantics without being aware of, or being able to state, the principles he is using.

Such principles are cognitive principles. We use them to understand our experience and to communicate on the basis of that understanding. But such metaphoric principles are not arbitrary, and they do not come out of nowhere. They are motivated by our knowledge of kinship and our everyday experience with it. Not just any kinship metaphor is consistent with that knowledge and that experience. Thus, the so-called free play of imagination is not, strictly speaking, free, though it is infinite. It is constrained by our knowledge, our experience, and our modes of cognition. And a violation of any given constraint, when successful, is meaningful precisely because the constraint exists.

Thus, the following questions arise:

— What, precisely, do we know about kinship?
— How does this knowledge give rise to the basic kinship metaphors?
— And how do these metaphors combine with that knowledge and with each other to give rise to the basic inference patterns that we use in inventing and understanding kinship metaphors?

2.2 Basic metaphors and Aristotle's metaphor

Discussions of metaphor often begin not with what I call basic conceptual metaphors, but rather with a supposed definition of metaphor. This 'definition' says that when two things share salient properties, one can be used as a metaphor for the other in order to evoke our recognition of some of those shared properties. Metaphor is thus *defined* as an expression of similarity. And the definition presupposes that the relevant properties that are shared and that constitute the similarity are already embodied in our conceptual representations. Metaphors, on this view, do not impose structure on our concepts; they merely rely on previous structure and do no more than highlight, filter, or select aspects of that given structure.

This supposed definition of metaphor is not a definition at all. As we shall see, it is itself a metaphor, a basic metaphor, but only one of a very great number. A metaphor, in general, provides a way of seeing one conceptual domain in terms of another conceptual domain. In fact, the sentence you just read is an instance of the basic conceptual metaphor: UNDERSTANDING IS SEEING. Cognition and vision are different, though related, domains of experience. Vision is structured in familiar and obvious ways. But understanding is something that must, itself, be understood and given structure in terms of some other domain. The UNDERSTANDING IS SEEING metaphor provides us with an appropriate domain, vision, for the comprehension of understanding itself. There is a reason why understanding is conventionally understood in terms of seeing and not scratching or bathing or flexing one's muscles or feeling the wind against one's follicles. Seeing is structured is a number of ways. What we see depends upon where we stand and where we direct our gaze. We can see clearly or hazily or through a glass darkly. The images that we see can be sharp or fuzzy. We can look at something with or without blinking, and when we do not want to see something, we can close our eyes. If our eyes are open, we normally see what is in front of them and not what is hidden from view. Seeing is thus a structured activity which is related to understanding in a systematic way, since a great deal of our information comes from seeing. It is the structure of seeing and its natural connection to understanding that gives rise to the UNDERSTANDING IS SEEING metaphor.

UNDERSTANDING IS SEEING is not just a relationship between two words or two simple concepts; rather it is a relationship between two conceptual domains, and it is a relationship with a highly articulated structure. It allows us to impose on the concept of understanding the structure that we have for vision. Thus, we can close our eyes to a problem, change our point of view, develop a new perspective on an issue, concentrate our focus or change it, see the big picture or attend to minute details, and so on.

It may seem as if closing our eyes and closing our eyes to a problem share properties. The reason they may seem to share properties is that we see one automatically as the other *because the* UNDERSTANDING IS SEEING *metaphor is so deeply entrenched in our conceptual systems.* But closing our eyes and closing our eyes to a problem do not share properties in any scientific sense. Thus metaphor is not just a matter of recognizing objectively preexisting shared properties. In many cases where we intuitively understand properties as being shared, they are shared by virtue of some metaphorical understanding.

Thus, when we understand something as having properties, those understood properties can be of two sorts: those properties arising from our knowledge of a domain in itself and those properties arising from seeing one domain metaphorically in terms of another. But in cases of very entrenched basic metaphors, like the UNDERSTANDING IS SEEING metaphor, on which we automatically rely, we do not feel these two types of properties to be distinguished.

The supposed definition of metaphor in terms of shared properties is thus actually just another basic metaphor. It can be expressed as A THING IS WHAT IT HAS SALIENT PROPERTIES OF. This might be called Aristotle's metaphor, since Aristotle has been interpreted as implying that the invention of metaphor is the recognition of objective properties' being objectively shared by objective referents in the objective world.

Aristotle's metaphor looks a bit odd as a basic conceptual metaphor because it has no fixed source domain (like seeing) and no fixed target domain (like understanding). This suggests that Aristotle's metaphor might reduce to hordes of other basic metaphors, each with its fixed source and target domains. This reduction might proceed along the following lines. Suppose an Englishman feels that England takes care of him, and that the concept *mother* has *takes care of* as a salient functional property. Then, by Aristotle's metaphor (A THING IS WHAT IT HAS SALIENT PROPERTIES OF), he can say "England is my mother."

But there is a different basic metaphor underlying "England is my mother." That basic metaphor is A NATION IS A PERSON. (This explains why a nation can have a backyard and friends, why it can extend its hand in friendship, and so on.) If England is a person, what sort of person is it? The kind that takes care of the Englishman: his mother. Therefore, he can say "England is my mother." Then Aristotle's metaphor has been reduced in this one specific case to a different basic metaphor, one with specific source and target domains. This basic metaphor, A NATION IS A PERSON, is overshadowed and obscured by the richly detailed and intimately known conceptual domain (people) with which it interacts to produce the specific metaphor. If such an analysis could be done for all instances of Aristotle's metaphor, then Aristotle's metaphor would be reduced from a basic metaphor to a generalization over all such cases.

How is it that Aristotle's metaphor can have been mistaken as a definition for all metaphor? Other basic metaphors often do creative work. They impose structure. They impose salient properties. Suppose a metaphor is so successful that the salient properties it imposes become entrenched in our conceptual representations. Then, in retrospect, the metaphor can look like an example of Aristotle's metaphor, since it equates two things that, in our conceptual representations, now share salient properties. But originally it is not an example of Aristotle's metaphor, because the salient properties that Aristotle's metaphor requires do not exist independently of the basic metaphor that imposed them. Aristotle's metaphor seems universal—and thus has obscured other basic metaphors—because creative metaphors, once established, can gradually become cases of Aristotle's metaphor. Many metaphors can look like examples of Aristotle's metaphor once they have done their work. And so Aristotle's metaphor has been used, mistakenly, to define all metaphor.

In fact, it is not from Aristotle's metaphor that interesting metaphors derive. Creative metaphors call for conceptual revision. They require us to reconceive the ontology of a thing. They entail the attribution of new salient properties, and thus *create* similarity. Suppose that a writer and reader share models of child as guileless and natural (or as irresponsible and emotionally temperamental, or whatever). Then for the writer to refer to a guileless, natural person as a child entails no conceptual revision. It is simply A THING (the person) IS WHAT IT HAS SALIENT PROPERTIES OF (child). Similarly, it is no longer inventive in English to call an unsophisticated and natural person a "child of Nature"; no conceptual revision is involved. It is sheerly an example of A THING IS WHAT IT HAS SALIENT PROPERTIES OF.

Suppose, however, that a writer sufficiently revises his concept of architecture to see how "Architecture is frozen music." Suppose he sufficiently revises his concept of the relation of childhood to adulthood to see how "The child is the father of the man." Then the reader must at least temporarily revise his concepts of architecture and the relation of childhood to adulthood in order to understand the metaphors. If the revision is not temporary but permanent, then thereafter the metaphors will be for the reader simply cases of A THING IS WHAT IT HAS SALIENT PROPERTIES OF. Thus, Aristotle's metaphor has seemed universal and all-encompassing.

There are, however, some metaphors that, no matter how entrenched and automatic they become, can never be taken as instances of Aristotle's metaphor because in no sense can they be seen as involving shared properties. Take for example the orientational metaphor MORE IS UP, which accounts for expressions such as "Stocks fell on the New York Exchange," "Congress has put a ceiling on funding for basic research," and so on. These are clearly metaphorical expressions which are not based on shared properties, and there are a wide variety of other such cases (see Lakoff and Johnson, 1980).

There are many basic metaphors besides Aristotle's, and some are much more interesting. Aristotle's metaphor is not specifically tied to the conceptual domain of kinship, but it interacts with other basic metaphors and commonplace notions that are specifically tied to kinship and through this combination helps to produce specific kinship metaphors. In the same way, there are other basic conceptual processes that are also independent of kinship and which also interact with our knowledge of kinship to yield kinship metaphors. Let us look at two of these general conceptual processes that combine with our specific knowledge of kinship to produce kinship metaphors: they are the "metonymy of associations" and a general basic metaphor PROPERTIES ARE PERSONS.

2.3 Metonymy of associations

A metonymy is a cognitive process wherein one thing closely related to another in a single conceptual domain is used to stand for that other thing. There are many types of metonymies. For example, one cocktail waitress might say to another "The whiskey sour won't leave me alone," thus referring to a customer by the order he was served. Similarly, when someone driving an Alfa Romeo cruises slowly back and forth past a sidewalk café, one female patron may say to another "The Alfa's out looking for a good time again." Here the car is standing for the driver.

One of the most common forms of metonymy depends on conventional cultural associations, such as the association of evil with darkness, health with nature, or innocence with children. Thus, when we speak of someone's "dark side," we can mean *metonymically* that it is an evil side, or *metaphorically* that it cannot be seen, that is, that we have no knowledge of it. Frequently, both senses are used to reinforce each other, since the unknown is often feared and seen as evil. Similarly, when food is spoken of as being "natural," it is taken as meaning that it is healthy, even though "natural" can also refer to natural poisons and carcinogens. The general principle governing such cases I will call the "metonymy of associations": A THING MAY STAND FOR WHAT IT IS CONVENTIONALLY ASSOCIATED WITH.

2.4 Personification of properties

We are people. We know a lot about ourselves. And we often make sense of other things by viewing them as people too. For example, we may view countries as people in sentences like "Greece and Turkey are not currently friends" and "Poland was raped by Germany." Such personification metaphors are common. One of the most basic of the personification metaphors is AN ABSTRACT PROPERTY IS A PERSON WHOSE SALIENT CHARACTERISTIC IS THAT

PROPERTY. In westerns, the white hats are pitted against
the black hats. Metonymically, we understand black for evil
and white for good, as well as the part (the hat) for the
whole (the person). Metaphorically, we understand the people (the good guys and the bad guys) as personifying the properties (good and evil). Here we see the logic of the interaction between metaphor and metonymy: If A STANDS FOR B
and B IS C metaphorically, then A STANDS FOR C. If a black
hat stands for the outlaw and the outlaw personifies evil,
then the black hat stands for evil.

2.5 Basic kinship metaphors

Let us now turn to kinship. We have various commonplace
notions about kinship in general and about specific kinship
roles. One very basic commonplace notion about kinship in
general is that, normally, children inherit salient characteristics of parents. Thus, when a child grows to be a foot taller
than either parent, it is a reportable occurrence because we
take it to be anomalous. The commonplace notion does not
hold that salient characteristics must be inherited, and we
typically hold the conflicting commonplace notion that a bad
child of good parents is a "bad seed." But the commonplace
notion does indicate that when parent and offspring share a
salient characteristic, then the offspring has inherited it. If
asked why a particular woman is level-headed, we might say,
"Well, she's her mother's daughter," meaning "Like mother,
like daughter." We are comfortable hearing Telemachus
called a "true son of Odysseus" because he shares his father's
capacity for (among other things) artifice, deception, and
lies. This is a commonplace notion of inheritance.

The commonplace notion of inheritance is a commonplace
notion about kinship. Although the personification of properties metaphor is quite general and not specifically about
kinship, it can combine with our commonplace notion of
inheritance to yield a basic kinship metaphor. The combination works like this: According to the personification of properties metaphor, AN ABSTRACT PROPERTY IS A PERSON
WHOSE SALIENT CHARACTERISTIC IS THAT PROPERTY. If it
can be a person, it can be a parent. By the commonplace
notion of inheritance, parents pass on their salient properties

to their children. What follows is the first basic kinship metaphor:

(1) AN ABSTRACT PROPERTY IS THE PARENT OF SOMETHING HAVING THAT PROPERTY.

Thus, (1) can be seen as arising from the following inference pattern: Personification of properties + people can be parents + inheritance => (1). Thus, for example, a *child of evil* has evil as a property and the abstract property evil as its parent.

The elements used in the inference pattern leading to (1) can also combine with the metonymy of associations to produce a close variant of (1). By the personification of properties, AN ABSTRACT PROPERTY *B* IS A PERSON WHOSE SALIENT CHARACTERISTIC IS THAT PROPERTY *B*. By the metonymy of associations, IF *A* IS CONVENTIONALLY ASSOCIATED WITH *B*, THEN *A* CAN STAND FOR *B*. Therefore, *A* IS A PERSON WHOSE SALIENT CHARACTERISTIC IS THE PROPERTY *B*. Then, since people can be parents, and, by inheritance, parents pass on their salient characteristics to offspring, *A* IS THE PARENT OF SOMETHING HAVING *B* AS A SALIENT CHARACTERISTIC. In general, IF *A* IS CONVENTIONALLY ASSOCIATED WITH ABSTRACT PROPERTY *B*, THEN *A* IS THE PARENT OF SOMETHING HAVING *B* AS A SALIENT CHARACTERISTIC. Thus, "sons of darkness" inherit the salient properties (evil among them) with which darkness is conventionally associated.

We also have the commonplace notions that a child, certainly during gestation, is part of the mother, and that the whole is made up of its parts. These two commonplace notions combine to yield the basic kinship metaphor

(2) THE WHOLE IS THE MOTHER OF THE PARTS.

This explains why nodes representing linguistic categories are called "mother nodes" (but not "father nodes"), and why those representing subcategories must be child nodes. But since such a child node also represents a category which may have subcategories, it must be a "daughter node" (rather than a "son node").

Our commonplace notion of kinship includes the very basic notion that children spring from their parents, and hence they are called "offspring." This motivates the basic kinship metaphor

(3) WHAT SPRINGS FROM SOMETHING IS ITS OFFSPRING.

For example, Italian springs from Latin. Therefore, Italian is the offspring of Latin. The arrow springs from the bow. Therefore, *Job* 41:20 calls the arrow the son of the bow.

This metaphor has three special cases. The first involves causation. Since effects spring from their causes,

(3a) CAUSES ARE PARENTS AND EFFECTS ARE
OFFSPRING.

For example, age is the mother of sickness.

The second special case also involves causation, and is an application of the first special case. We have in our commonplace notions of causation (and often in our scientific theories of causation) the basic metaphor that

(4) CONDITIONS ARE CAUSES AND RESULTS ARE
EFFECTS.

This concerns causation, and not kinship. However, it interacts with (3a) to yield a basic kinship metaphor.

(3a+4) CONDITIONS ARE PARENTS AND RESULTS ARE
OFFSPRING.

We also have the basic metaphor that

(5) THE SUBSEQUENT THING SPRINGS FROM THE INITIAL
THING.

(3) combines with (5) to yield:

(3+5) THE SUBSEQUENT THING IS THE OFFSPRING OF
THE INITIAL THING.

An example of (3a+4) is "Filth is the mother of stench." Filth is a condition which results in stench. So filth is a cause, and stench is its result. Therefore, filth is a parent whose offspring is stench.

An example of (3+5) is "May, that modr is of monthes glade" (happy months). In England, May is the first full month of good weather after a hard winter.* Other months

*In medieval French courtly poetry, which influenced Chaucer, a

of spring are subsequent. Therefore, the other months of spring are May's offspring.

According to our commonplace notions of kinship, groups of siblings have two kinds of properties. First, by our commonplace notion of inheritance, siblings each have the salient characteristics of their parents. Therefore, it is a property of a group of siblings that the members share inherited salient characteristics. Second, groups of siblings have functional properties: family loyalty, common cultural background, and so on. According to Aristotle's metaphor, A THING IS WHAT IT HAS SALIENT CHARACTERISTICS OF. Thus, a group whose members share salient properties— whether properties inherited by individuals or functional properties of the group—is metaphorically a group of siblings. Therefore,

(6) MEMBERS OF A NATURAL GROUP ARE SIBLINGS.

An example is "Death is the brother of sleep," where death and sleep are seen as similar states of inactivity. A different example is "brothers in distress," where the members of the group are like siblings not because they share a common inherent feature, but rather because they function as brothers, behaving loyally toward each other in the face of a common danger.

Lastly, we know that the first sibling on the scene is the oldest. Given that similar things are siblings, it follows that

(7) A PRIOR RELATED THING IS AN OLDER SIBLING.

For example, if we see darkness as related to but prior to light, we can call darkness "light's elder brother."

2.6 The basic metaphoric inference patterns

These basic kinship metaphors, in combination with more general basic metaphors such as Aristotle's and with commonplace notions, yield ten basic metaphoric inference

---

poem frequently begins with an evocation of spring, and the standard substitute for spring is May. In English, from *The Canterbury Tales* to *The Wasteland*, April is standard for the transition from winter to spring. "April showers bring May flowers."

patterns. There is a wide range of "x is kin of y" metaphors in English, such as "Necessity is the mother of invention." These ten metaphoric inference patterns account for how all such specific metaphors are understood.

(1) *Property transfer.* We associate properties with each kinship role. Some of these properties are inherent, and some are functional. For example, a mother has the inherent property of being female and the functional property of nurturing. If we call someone a child, we are calling him childlike. This is *property transfer.* A kinship metaphor of the form "x is kin of y" equates x with the kinship role. Therefore, it can transfer some of the properties we associate with the kin role to x. Thus, in "Tharmas, child of tears," Tharmas is characterized, via *property transfer,* as childlike. (Additionally, the particular childlike property, that of weeping, arises via *inheritance,* since tears are the parent who bequeathes the abstract property.) *Property transfer* is an application of Aristotle's metaphor. If something has a property we associate with a kinship role, then, by Aristotle's metaphor, it is that kinship role. If Tharmas is childlike, then he is a child. The transferred functional property is very often a treatment, behavior, or function of a kin relation, as in "He was a child of all the dale—he lived / Three months with one, and six months with another." The "he" is being cared for, a way in which, according to our conceptual models, children are typically treated. Frequently, I will say that we understand that something is metaphorically a child because we understand that it is *treated-as* a child, or *behaves-as* a child, or *functions-as* a child. All of these are special cases of functional *property transfer.*

(2) *Similarity.* By the basic metaphor (1) AN ABSTRACT PROPERTY IS THE PARENT OF SOMETHING HAVING THAT PROPERTY, we know that if two things share an inherent property then they have the same parent, and hence are siblings. We understand "Death is the brother of sleep" as implying that

death and sleep are similar because they share the property of inactivity. This is one special case of the basic metaphor (6) MEMBERS OF A NATURAL GROUP ARE SIBLINGS.

(3) *Group.* In our commonplace notions, groups of siblings have functional properties. Any other group having those functional properties is, by Aristotle's metaphor, a group of siblings. This inference pattern is also a special case of the basic metaphor (6) MEMBERS OF A NATURAL GROUP ARE SIBLINGS. (The more general basic metaphor MEMBERS OF A NATURAL GROUP ARE LATERAL RELATIVES accounts for the use of marital relations to indicate *grouping.*)

(4) *Inheritance.* x inherits a salient quality of y, as in "They are villaines, and the sonnes of darkness." This inference pattern derives as follows. According to basic metaphor (1), AN ABSTRACT PROPERTY IS THE PARENT OF SOMETHING HAVING THAT PROPERTY, and IF *A* IS CONVENTIONALLY ASSOCIATED WITH *B*, THEN *A* IS THE PARENT OF SOMETHING HAVING PROPERTY *B*. Therefore, the kinship role (sons) inherits properties of y, or properties associated with y. Then by *property transfer*, x has those properties. Thus, if darkness is associated with evil, then sons of darkness inherit evil, and the villains are evil.

(5) *Components or contents.* The components or contents of something can be its offspring, as in "The days of life are sisters." This inference pattern derives from the basic metaphor (2) THE WHOLE IS THE MOTHER OF THE PARTS. There is a special case of this inference pattern that derives from a very general part-whole metaphor, according to which the whole is understood as a container for its parts. Since THE WHOLE IS A CONTAINER and THE WHOLE IS THE MOTHER OF THE PARTS, therefore THE WHOLE IS A CONTAINER WHICH IS THE MOTHER OF THE PARTS. For example, arrows can be the "children of the quiver."

(6) *Order and succession.* Lateral relations can be modified to indicate precedence of birth and hence temporal or logical precedence, as in "Darknesse, lights elder brother." This derives from (7) A PRIOR RELATED THING IS AN OLDER SIBLING. The leading term of a series can also be the generator, as in "May, that modr is of monthes glade." This derives from the basic metaphor (3a+5) THE SUBSEQUENT THING IS THE OFFSPRING OF THE INITIAL THING.

Several metaphoric inference patterns derive at least in part from the basic metaphor (3) WHAT SPRINGS FROM SOMETHING IS ITS OFFSPRING. It would be inaccurate to say that these inference patterns are special cases of (3), since other basic metaphors may also underlie them.

(7) *Causation as progeneration.* The kinship term indicates a causal link between x and y, as in "stench, diseases, and old filth, their mother." (This complex and subtle inference pattern is the subject of chapter 4.) This inference pattern derives from the basic metaphor (3+4) CONDITIONS ARE PARENTS AND RESULTS ARE OFFSPRING.

(8) *Biological resource as parent.* Biological products spring from biological resources. According to (3), WHAT SPRINGS FROM SOMETHING IS ITS OFF-SPRING. Therefore, biological products are offspring of biological resources. For example, the earth can be the mother and the sun the father of trees.

(9) *Place and time as parent.* Location and situation (usually place and time) give birth to occupants, as in "mid-May's eldest child, / The coming musk-rose." This inference pattern derives from various basic metaphors. According to (1), IF *A* IS CONVENTION-ALLY ASSOCIATED WITH ABSTRACT PROPERTY *B*, THEN *A* IS THE PARENT OF SOMETHING HAVING *B* AS A SALIENT CHARACTERISTIC. Therefore, if a place or time (e.g., Babylon) is associated with a property (e.g., wickedness), then offspring of the place have that property as a salient characteristic (e.g., children of Babylon are wicked). According to

(3a+4), CONDITIONS ARE PARENTS AND RESULTS ARE OFFSPRING. A place or time has conditions. Occupants of the place or time can be understood as springing from those conditions. Therefore, they are offspring of the place or time. According to (2), THE WHOLE IS THE MOTHER OF THE PARTS. Occupants of a place or time can be understood as parts of the place or time. "I need to get back to Chicago" can be understood as meaning "I need to get back to various occupants of Chicago." Therefore, the place or time is the mother of the occupants.

(10) *Lineage in the world, the mind, and behavior.* Kinship metaphor is perhaps most revealing and illuminating in its aptitude to model mental events. Kinship metaphors can indicate what components of the world, the mind, and behavior are allowed to affect others. I call this *lineage.* Just how they do this is the subject of a lengthy discussion later in this chapter. This inference pattern is a pure application of WHAT SPRINGS FROM SOMETHING IS ITS OFF-SPRING to the domain of the interactions between the mind and the world and behavior.

Coherences of the metaphoric inference patterns

In our mental models of kinship, we blend the vertical, the lateral, and the hierarchical. Lateral can always suggest vertical (brothers share a parent), and vertical often suggests lateral (a mother of two things implies a sibling relation). Lateral *similarity* can imply a common vertical *inheritance*, and both *inheritance* and *similarity* are metaphors for the basic process of *property transfer*. This multivalence makes kinship metaphor rich in capacity to capture complex interconnection. The natural blending in the domain of kinship produces natural blendings of the metaphoric inference patterns:

— *Similarity* and *inheritance* cohere when laterally related things are *similar* because of common *inheritance*, as in "Graces, daughters of delight."

— *Similarity, lineage,* and *group* cohere when behaviors or feelings, *similar* in having the same mental source, are *grouped* by lateral relation as concomitants, as in "After Glotonye thanne comth Lecherie, for these two synnes been so ny cosyns that ofte tyme they wol nat departe" and "Gambling is the brother of iniquity."

— *Place and time as parent* and *inheritance* cohere when a *place and time* location that connotes a civilization or ideology or behavior produces an occupant who *inherits* components of the ideology, as in "I am a child of the modern era."

— *Place and time as parent, functional property transfer, biological resource as parent, inheritance,* and *causation* very frequently cohere. When a *place and time* location nurtures an occupant beneficially and biologically, the location can assume the role of generalized parent, *behaving-as* parent toward the occupant, its child, who is *treated-as* its child, and who often *inherits.* The location is seen as having *caused* (in the sense of progenerated) the occupant, as in "He was a child of all the dale."

— *Place and time as parent* and *lineage* cohere when a *place and time* location is also a world situation (like "night") affecting feelings or behavior, as in "Night is the mother of melancholy."

— *Lineage* draws on both *causation* and *similarity,* in the sense that it can be a special case of either. One thing in the world, the mind, or behavior can spring from another such thing because of causation. Two such things can be laterally related because they are similar.

Constraints

It might seem as if kinship metaphors are symmetric, making, for example, "x is parent of y" equivalent to "y is child of x." But there are constraints on the symmetry:

— Connotations. Different kin terms evoke different connotations, as I discuss in section 2.7. When certain connotations of a specific kin relation are desired, the inverse relation cannot be used. This is always the case with *property transfer:* "Tharmas, child of tears" is not equivalent to "Tears, parents of Tharmas." Certain inference patterns are connected with certain connotations. Since children *inherit, inheritance* always requires an offspring term. (Also, it may be that the offspring term strongly suppresses the "bad seed" connotations in favor of the "inheritance" connotations, and that the parent term is somewhat more ambiguous in this regard.) All examples I have found of *biological resource as parent* require a parent term. *Place and time as parent* requires an offspring term except when thematic or logical concerns override it, as in "Babylon is the mother of harlots and abominations."

— Thematics. I will not make the argument here, but I have observed that in analogical constructions in English, the heir of meaning typically comes first. I call this rubric "heir-first." Kinship metaphor is constrained by heir-first: "Accuracy is the twin brother of honesty" is not equivalent to "Honesty is the twin brother of accuracy."

— Logic. Inverse relations can imply different quantifications. "Paula is the mother of brats" and "Brats are children of Paula" imply different quantifications. The second suggests that all brats derive from Paula; the first suggests only that some brats come from Paula—there may be other mothers of brats. This carries over into kinship metaphor: "Solitude is the mother of anxieties" and "Anxieties are children of solitude" suggest different quantifications.

Later on, I will present other constraints on kinship metaphors that derive either from connotations of particular choices for x and y or from specifics of *lineage*.

Details of the metaphoric inference patterns

PROPERTY TRANSFER

Consider Blake's "Why weepest thou, Tharmas, child of tears in the bright house of joy?" Remember that the underlying form is schematized as x = kin of y. Here, x = Tharmas, kin = child, and y = tears. This kinship term transfers some of its meaning to x: Tharmas is being characterized as childlike in his emotional reactions.

Wordsworth's "wooed the artless daughter of the hills" characterizes the girl as daughterlike, as young, feminine, dependent, cared for, exemplifying *property transfer.*

In cases where the kinship term is both lateral and symmetric, like "sisters" or "twin brother," as in "Accuracy is the twin brother of honesty," then there is also *property transfer* possible to the object y.

Certain stereotypical treatments, behaviors, and functions attach to each member of a family. These are functional properties and can be transferred. A child is cared for, sheltered. A stepchild is abused. A kinship term can be used metaphorically to give its stereotypical treatment to something else and thus to indicate that something is treated in a certain way: "He was a child of all the dale—he lived / Three months with one, and six months with another" (Wordsworth) and "The navy has been the stepchild of both parliaments" (OED).

Similarly, something that behaves a certain way or performs a certain function can be expressed by the kinship term to which the behavior or function attaches. A wife, for instance, in various alternative stereotypes, characteristically limits freedom, provides reliable and comfortable companionship, or elicits devoted and attentive care. Hence "Wife: a fetter fixed to one leg" (OED); "The pipe is the bachelor's wife" (OED); and "His wooden wife, as he sometimes called his ship" (OED). Fortune and time have served in place of a mother to Oedipus, and hence he calls Fortune his mother and the months (waxing and waning moons) his brothers: ἐγὼ δ' ἐμαυτὸν παῖδα τῆς Τύχης νέμων / . . . / τῆς γὰρ πέφυκα μητρός· οἱ δὲ συγγενεῖς / μῆνές με μικρὸν καὶ μέγαν διώρισαν (Sophocles). Uncles take care of nieces and nephews intermittently; they can be called on in a crisis: hence "Uncle Sam" and the use of "uncle" to mean "pawnbroker" (OED). Milton describes the angels as "sons of one great Sire / Hymning th'Eternal Father" whom God calls, for their behavior, "my Sons."

Stepmothers and stepfathers are consistently seen as having no function other than cruelty, abuse, neglect, and destruction:

Invention, Nature's child, fled stepdame Study's blows. (Sidney)

What a tragic, treacherous stepdame is vulgar Fortune to her children. (Carlyle, OED)

My dul wit is hindred by stepmother of foryeting. (OED)

The Step-moder of vertu, And ful enemy to cryst ihesu, Which called ys 'Prosperyte.' (Lydgate, OED)

Flattery, Which is the stepmother called . . . To all.*

Kings, if they be Wise for themselves, will be Nursing Fathers, not Stepfathers.

(More examples in appendix 2A.)

These all derive from the prototypical connotation of "step" in Menander's "There is no more terrible evil than a stepmother."

SIMILARITY

Lateral relations can indicate *similarity*. Sometimes this *similarity* is wholly or partially specified, as in the following examples:

Sparta in laws and institutions is the sister of Crete. (Jowett, OED)

A clear stream flowing with a muddy one, / Till in its wayward current it absorbs . . . The vexed eddies of its wayward brother. (Tennyson)

Hark how the Bells upon the waters play
Their sister-tunes, from Thames his either side. (Jonson)

Ah, brother of the brief but blazing star! (Emerson)

(More examples in appendix 2B.)

We saw an example earlier where Oedipus called the months (the changing moons) his brothers because he, too, waxes and wanes.

More often, the similarity is left for the understander to supply:

---

*Unless otherwise noted, all examples are attested. Examples for which I give no citation are, though attested, either anonymous or unauthenticated by me.

Other diseases, neere cousins to the plague (Cogan, OED)

Heere's the twyn-brother of thy Letter. (Shakespeare)

He has a sin of mine, he its near brother. (Hopkins)

There was peace after death, the brother of sleep. (Stevens)

Faire speche that is feithles is falsnes brother. (Langland, OED)

That April Morn, of this the very brother (Wordsworth)

Eek Plato seith, whoso that kan hym rede,
The wordes moote be cosyn to the dede. (Chaucer)

Now wyll I proue ye a lyar
Next cosyne to a friar. (Bale, OED)

(More examples in appendix 2C.)

GROUP

Lateral relations often indicate a natural *grouping*. This frequently coheres with the *behaves-as* inference pattern, a special case of *functional property transfer*. For instance, "Partners in faith, and brothers in distress" (Wordsworth) implies both a natural *grouping* and that the partners *behave* toward each other in brotherly fashion. The five branches of the rose's calyx are called "brothers." Here are some other examples:

If music and sweet poetry agree, . . . the sister and the brother (Shakespeare)

Gibble Gabble, The Wife of Inflammable Gass (Blake)

Brothers in soul! through distant times (Wordsworth)

> The youth elect
> Must do the thing, or both will be destroyed.
> "Then," cried the young Endymion, overjoy'd
> "We are twin brothers in this destiny." (Keats)

(More examples in appendix 2D.)

INHERITANCE

Often, metaphors of the form "kin of y" mean simply that the kinship term inherits the property y, or a property with which y is associated. By *property transfer*, this property then belongs to x.

Emerson's "sons of contradiction" means "people with a penchant for contradiction"; the penchant for contradiction is the governing characteristic. Lawrence's "child of innocence" means "innocent person." Wordsworth's "daughter of affliction" means "afflicted woman." Johnson's "daughter of perfection" means "perfect woman." In Jonson's "the child of Ignorance . . . I," "child" inherits "ignorance" and transfers it to "I."

Scriptural expressions like "child of wrath," "child of disobedience," and "child of anger" all exemplify *inheritance* of a characteristic, as do the following examples:

Invention, nature's child (Sidney)

Natives of poverty, children of malheur (Stevens)

They are villaines, and the sonnes of darkness. (Shakespeare)

(More examples in appendix 2E.)

Beliefs are also inherited:

Elizabeth . . . was a child of the Italian Renascence. (OED)

Came home and took a pipe after supper with landlord, who is a staunch son of liberty. (J. Adams, OED)

[Voltaire and Rousseau], frozen sons of the feminine tabernacle of Bacon, Newton, and Locke (Blake)

Rousseau, Jean Jacques: French man of letters, Geneva-born, enigmatic child of the Age of Reason, and father of the Romantic Age. (Crane Brinton)

(More examples in appendix 2F.)

This last example illustrates that beliefs can be both *inherited* from and bequeathed to an age.

Often, *inheritance* of characteristics dovetails with *inheritance* of beliefs, as in the Scriptural "children of God," "child of truth," "child of wisdom," and the following examples:

As a child of the modern era, I believe that there are all sorts of physical regularities. (John Searle)

If you think there is nothing problematic or mysterious about a symbol system solving problems, you are a child of

today, whose views have been formed since mid-century.
(Allen Newell and Herbert A. Simon)

Virtue is the daughter of Heaven. (Pound)

(More examples in appendix 2G.)

COMPONENTS OR CONTENTS

The *components or contents* of a thing are frequently
offspring of the thing. This metaphoric inference pattern
often combines with *place and time as parent*. Consider
"Soon—as when summer of his sister spring / Crushes and
tears the rare enjewelling" (Hopkins). The summer and
spring, which are *components or contents* of the year, are
therefore the laterally related offspring of the year. Similarly,
"Daughters of Time, the hypocrite Days" (Emerson) and
"The days of life are sisters" (OED) make offspring out of
components or contents of time and life. "May" is both a
component of "spring" and the result of *place and time as
parent* in "When a sister, born for each strong month-
brother / Spring's one daughter, the sweet child May, / Lies
in the breast of the young year-mother" (Hopkins). Donne
uses "children of his quiver" as a metaphor for arrows. The
arrows are contents of the quiver, and therefore, by virtue of
the *contents* inference pattern, offspring of the quiver.

ORDER AND SUCCESSION

Precedence of birth can indicate temporal precedence:

Darknesse, lights elder brother, his birth-right
Claims o'r this world, and to heaven hath chased light.
(Donne)

The art of roasting or rather broiling (which I take to be
the elder brother) (Lamb, OED)

Venice, the eldest Child of Liberty (Wordsworth)

And the leading term of a series can be the generator, as in
the lines, "In May, that moder is of monthes glade"
(Chaucer).

CAUSATION

Kinship generation can be used to express *causation as
progeneration*. As I explain in chapter 4, causation is never

portrayed in cases of kinship metaphor as mere invariant sequence, as mere regularity. It is always a necessary connection. The necessary connection is not determinism, but rather nondeterministic efficacy, as I will explain. Consider:

sickenesses, or their true mother, Age (Donne)

and

stench, diseases, and old filth, their mother (Jonson)

In both examples, the cause and the effects (age causes sickness; filth causes disease and stench) are necessarily connected because there is some power, some efficacy in the cause to produce the effect. This is quite at variance with causation as constant conjunction. Indeed, age does not invariably produce sickness, or filth disease.

Language and knowledge have genealogies under *causation as progeneration* in

Italian, eldest daughter of ancient Latin

and

Natural philosophy, that great mother of sciences.

"The child is the father of the man" (Wordsworth) maps the father-to-child progeneration onto the child-to-man transformation to illuminate the second in terms of the first. The causation is progenerative; there is a necessary connection between child and man.

Causation also covers the metaphysical cosmogony typical of mythologies, as in "Some say the Light was father of the Night / And some, the Night was father of the Light" (Tennyson).

Causation as progeneration can overlap with *causation as activity, institution, and invention* in cases like

George Washington was the father of his country.

England is the mother of Parliaments.

The Duke of Exeter's daughter, Scavenger's daughter: names given to instruments of torture of which the invention is attributed to the Duke of Exeter and Sir W. Skevington. (OED)

BIOLOGICAL RESOURCE AS PARENT

There is an understanding of nature in which reproduction constitutes only one kind of *biological resource as parent*. The preexisting biological material and states necessary for growth or other processes are also seen as generators, as in "mother Earth," "mother Sea," and "mother Nature," and the following examples:

Aristotle sayth that the erthe is moder and the sonne fader of trees. (OED)

stench, diseases, and old filth, their mother (Jonson)

the earth, great mother of us all (Spenser)

Water . . . was by some thought to be the Mother of Earth. (OED)

PLACE AND TIME AS PARENT

This inference pattern captures our understanding of place and time—even of location and situation in their broadest meanings—as giving birth to their occupants. Consider Spenser's "That daintie Rose, the daughter of her Morne." *Property transfer* characterizes the rose as feminine and young or undeveloped. *Place and time as parent* characterizes "daintie Rose" as the child of morning. Similarly, Keats writes "And mid-May's eldest child, / The coming muskrose."

"Daughters of Time, the Hypocrite Days" (Emerson) and "The days of life are sisters" (OED) exemplify *place and time as parent*.

The *inheritance* inference pattern combines with *place and time as parent* in:

Whispered the Muse in Saadi's cot:
O gentle Saadi, listen not,
Tempted by thy praise of wit,
Or by thirst and appetite
For the talents not thine own,
To sons of contradiction.
Never, son of eastern morning,
Follow falsehood, follow scorning. (Emerson)

Here, "son of eastern morning" implies that the East, as a place, produced Saadi, but also that he inherits Eastern, in contradistinction to Western, ways of thinking. The *inheritance* of beliefs from an epoch often combines with *place and time as parent*, as in "Kant: good child of the Age of Reason." When Herrick uses "sons of summer" as a metaphor for "harvesters," it implies *place and time as parent* as well as *inheritance* of summer qualities. Milton's reference to angels as sons of Heaven combines *inheritance* with *place and time as parent*. Wordsworth's "And wooed the artless daughter of the hills" implies first that the person is young, a dependent girl—this is *property transfer*—, second that the hill somehow produced her—this is *place and time as parent*—, and third that she inherited qualities of naturalness and rusticity—this is *inheritance*. Blake's "Contemplation, daughter of the grey morning" combines *place and time as parent* and *inheritance*, as does Daniel's "Care-charmer sleepe, son of the sable night." Blake's "Children of the Spring" as a metaphor for the lotus flowers on the water blends *place and time as parent* and something close to *biological resource as parent*, depending on whether spring is a time or a certain biological condition of the world. Spenser calls the sun "daughter of the day." Some other examples of *place and time as parent* are "Babylon is the mother of harlots and abominations" (Rev. 17:5), Carlyle's "As an actually existing Son of time, look at what time did bring" (OED), Shakespeare's "Every minute now should be the Father of some Strategm," Donne's "Daughters of London," for unmarried girls in London, Dylan Thomas's "Deep with the first dead lies London's daughter," and Newman's "I'm the son of the prairie and the wind that sweeps the plain."

Freud, in "Revision of Dream Theory," combines *place and time as parent* and *inheritance*. "This one repudiated thought, however, or, properly speaking, this one impulse, is the child of night; it belongs to the dreamer's unconscious and on that account it is repudiated and rejected by him. It had to wait for the nightly relaxation of repression in order to arrive at any kind of expression." The conditions of night allow the thought to surface—this is *place and time as parent;*

but the thought also *inherits* connotations of night as dark and related to dreams and the unconscious. Aeschylus similarly has the Eumenides call themselves the "gloomy, everlasting children of the night" (ἡμεῖς γάρ ἐσμεν Νυκτὸς αἰανῆ τέκνα) and "unlucky, woeful daughters of night" (κόραι δυστυχεῖς Νυκτὸς).

Wordsworth uses negation of *place and time as parent* to indicate that something is beyond time in "Thou art not a Child of Time, / But Daughter of the Eternal Prime!"

Place and time as parent frequently cannot be distinguished from *inheritance* of both qualities and beliefs. The Scriptural "children of the East," "children of the world," "children of the day," "child of the age," and so on. exemplify this blend. Here are some other examples:

Children of Summer!
Ye fresh Flowers that brave (Wordsworth)

Monday's child is fair of face,
Tuesday's child is full of grace.

You are the child of the universe.
You have a right to be here. (Gibran)

LINEAGE (IN THE WORLD, THE MIND, AND BEHAVIOR)

The principal use of kinship metaphor is to express the paths by which things in the world, the mind, and behavior can spring from each other. Usually, these expressions concern how mind affects itself, how world affects mind, and how mind affects behavior. As I will explain in chapter 4, apparently our conceptions of mental causation and creation conform very well to causation as progeneration but very badly to other concepts of causation.

What order can be found in the myriad examples of kinship metaphor that express some lineage of events, states, or properties in the world, mind, and behavior? Suppose we simply list a few pairs of parents and offspring we find in kinship metaphor:

Parent	Offspring
night	fear
despair	madness
fear	cruelty
avarice	gambling
wish	thought
fear	superstition
celerity	good fortune

Such a list of twenty pairs once suggested to me a basic model that I have found to be repeatedly verified and extended by scores of other such pairs. (Note that I am not modeling mind here, but rather presenting a model I claim speakers of English share as a basis of communication. This does not imply that they believe the model.)

What are the components of this model? Every x and every y falls into one of three major categories: World (W), Mind (M), or Behavior (B). World is not only physical reality, but also situations and circumstances in which Mind finds itself. World can affect Mind. Mind can affect Behavior. And Behavior can affect World:

World → Mind

Mind → Behavior

Behavior → World

Mind has components. The dominant component in kinship metaphors is Feeling (F). We almost always find the three links above occurring as

World → Feeling

Feeling → Behavior

Behavior → World

The connection between Feeling and Behavior is so strong that English often merges them: feeling angry and behaving angrily can both be nominalized into "anger" ("Anger paralyzed my reason" vs. "His anger was offensive"). So when a feeling and a behavior have the same nominalization, then W→F can also appear to be W→B, and F→B can also appear to be B→B. I will explain these later when I come to concatenations like W→(F→)B, and when I examine the internal structures of F and B.

Let us look at some evidence for each of these three major links.

World → Feeling

Till Sable Night, mother of dread and fear (Shakespeare)

The moon is the mother of pathos and pity. (Stevens)

Night thou foule Mother of annoyance sad (Spenser)

Solitude is the mother of anxieties. (P. Syrus, trans. Lyman).

All things doe willingly in change delight,
The fruitfull mother of our appetite:
Rivers the clearer and more plesing are,
Where their fair spreading streames run wide and farr;
And a dead lake that no strange bark doth greet,
Corrupts itself and what doth live in it. (Donne)

If my dear love were but the child of State (Shakespeare)

(*Property transfer* in the first three examples also characterizes night as feminine, with connotations of mysticism and emotion.)

Feeling → Behavior

If your Highness keep
Your purport, you will shock him even to death,
Or baser courses, children of despair. (Tennyson)

Enterprise! Daughter of Hope! her favourite Child!
Whom she to young Ambition bore (Wordsworth)

Then [Self Love] bore a daughter called emulation, who married honour. (Blake)

The true child of vanity is violence. (δυσσεβίας μὲν ὕβρις / τέκος ὡς ἐτύμως) (Aeschylus)

Fear, father of cruelty (Pound)

certainty / mother and nurse of repose (Pound)

When Mischiefe is the child of Mirthe (Feltham, OED)

Contentment shares the desolate domain
With Independence, child of high Disdain. (Wordsworth)

(In this example, independence as Behavior and as Feeling are not distinguished.)

> And great with child of mischief travaild long (Spenser)

> The noble hart, that harbours vertuous thought,
> And is with child of glorious great intent,
> Can neuer rest, until it forth haue brought
> Th'eternall brood of glorie excellent. (Spenser)

> The mother of such magnificence (they think) is but only a proude ambitious desire to be spoken of farre and wide. (Hooker, OED)

> Ydelness, modr of all vices (OED)

(If vice is seen as Behavior, then this is Feeling affecting Behavior.)

> Sweet Smile, the daughter of the Queene of Love (Spenser)

(Here, "Queen of Love" can mean "love," an example of a split Brooke-Rose [1965] has analyzed as "pure attribution.")

> Love to money is moder of passing mych yuel. (Pecock, OED)

> Thou pain the onely guest of loath'd constraint,
> The child of curse, man's weakness foster-child,
> Brother to woe, and father of complaint (Sidney)

(Here, pain, a Feeling, generates complaint, a type of Behavior, i.e. linguistic production.)

> Purposelessness is the mother of crime.

> Gambling is the child of avarice.

Behavior → World

> Trade is the mother of money.

> Toil is the father of fame.

> Diligence is the mother of good luck.

> Celerity is the mother of good fortune.

Wordsworth addresses Kilchurn castle as "child of loud-throated war." War, a kind of Behavior, led to the existence of the castle, a change in the World situation. No doubt that suffices for first-level understanding. But we will explore this further when we come to concatenations.

The three links W→F, F→B, and B→W may suggest behaviorist notions of stimulus and response. But the dominant link in the model is in fact mind affecting itself:

Mind → Mind

This is often specifically

Feeling → Feeling

But not all of Mind is Feeling in this model. There are also Thoughts and Knowledge, which combine into Intellect. We find that Feelings can affect Intellect and vice versa:

Feeling → Intellect

Intellect → Feeling

Let us look at the evidence for these last three links:

Feeling → Feeling

(Since Behavior reflects Feeling and language often merges them, as in "cowardice," "jealousy," "sloth," and "madness," F→F can cohere with F→B.)

Envye and Ire maken bitternesse in herte, which bitternesse is moder of Accidie [sloth]. (Chaucer)

For 'tis despaire that is the mother of madness. (Jonson, OED)

loves extremity . . . the father of fowle gealosy (Spenser)

Love-without-weakness . . . Of Genius sire and son (Emerson)

In this last example, genius can be emotional, visionary, Blakean, psychological, in addition to intellectual. The inverse kinship relations indicate that either Feeling promotes the other.

There is a special case of this category: a physiological feeling can be required for a certain psychological feeling:

Morpheus, the lively son of deadly sleepe (Sidney)

Dreames, which are the children of an idle brane (Shakespeare)

The underlying concept in these two examples seems to be that a given situation can lead to a certain Behavior by whatever occupies the situation. This is related to *place and time as parent*. Both rely on the basic metaphor (3) WHAT SPRINGS FROM SOMETHING IS ITS OFFSPRING.

Feeling → Intellect

Thy wish was father to that thought. (Shakespeare)

O hateful error, melancholy's child!
Why dost thou show, to the apt thoughts of men,
The things that are not? (Shakespeare)

Intellect → Feeling

Hatred is the child of misunderstanding.

Hate and mistrust are the children of blindness.

This completes the final list of direct connections of the basic model:

World → Feeling

Feeling → Behavior

Behavior → World

Feeling → Feeling

Feeling → Intellect

Intellect → Feeling

Thought and Feeling, agile, active, and changeable in the short term, are the dominant core of Mind in this model. Kinship metaphors present them virtually as the engine through which any generation involving mind must pass. Kinship metaphors mention much less frequently those components of mind it models as more stable over the long term. These are:

— Belief (L)
— Knowledge (K), which is part of Intellect
— Character (C), the durable psychological substrate of Feeling
— Regimen (R), long-term patterns of behavior

Of these, Belief occurs often. Its addition to the model gives what I call the "extended basic model." The other three occur so rarely that they may be taken as idiosyncratic extensions by various authors. All four have blurred and fuzzy boundaries with sporadic clear marks. Kinship metaphor upholds the naive distinction between knowledge and belief, and is usually content with the naive view of cognition as processing (Thought) of stored data (Knowledge). The new links in the extended basic model are:

Feeling → Belief

Intellect → Belief

The other links I have found are:

Character → Character

Character → Feeling

Regimen → Character

Thought → Knowledge

Here are the details:

Feeling → Belief

Fear has been the original parent of superstition. (Gibbon)

Religion: A daughter of Hope and Fear (Ambrose Bierce)

Intellect → Belief

Admiration is the daughter of ignorance.

There is an admiration which is the daughter of knowledge. (Joubert)

Prejudice is the child of ignorance. (Hazlitt)

Ignorance is the mother of suspicion.

Character → Character

O son, thou hast not true humility,
The highest virtue, mother of them all. (Tennyson)

Character → Feeling

This nobel passion, child of integrity (Shakespeare)

Regimen → Character

Fortitude is the child of Enterprise. (Wordsworth)

I take this to mean that enterprising behavior over time gradually influences character ("Habit, that all-consuming monster . . ."). Plausibly, it could mean rather that a momentary spurt of enterprise gives one the fortitude to confront the moment.

Thought → Knowledge

thought mother of science (Sidney)

his theory . . . child of his brains (Hopkins)

If we combine the links, we have:

the basic model:

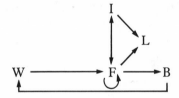

the extended basic model:

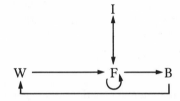

further plausible extensions:

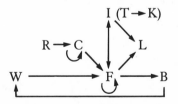

These graphs prompt three questions: (1) Are there missing links? Can World affect Thought? Can Belief affect Feeling or Behavior? (2) Are there concatenations? Since World can affect Feeling, and Feeling can affect Behavior, should we not find cases where World affects Behavior? (3) Should there not be a role for lateral relations in this model?

Missing links: constraints and lacunae. Are there links between world, mind, and behavior that genealogy does not fit well? Consider "The appearance of the comet set me thinking." This implies W-->I. (A dashed arrow indicates a possible link for which there is no attested kinship metaphor.) I have found two data that might suggest W-->I:

Imagination, daughter of sight

O Sacred, Wise, and Wisdom-giving Plant, / Mother of Science [said of the forbidden tree by Satan] (Milton)

But imagination and wisdom, rather than clear components of Intellect, suggest multiple interactions between various components of Mind. So though W-->I appears to have a sure place in the model, it has not proven its place in kinship metaphor.

Consider the unattested phrases:

My new idea set me running.

Learning that new chemical principle was the father of my new lab technique.

Such phrases underdetermine the link needed to handle them. They could be either I→(F→)B or I-->B.

Consider the unattested phrases:

Prejudice is the father of cruelty.

Religious belief is the mother of good works.

These could be either L→(F→)B or L-->B.

Consider the unattested phrases:

Myth is the mother of science.

Religion is the mother of ignorance.

Faith is the mother of proof.

The ease of these phrases makes it surprising that I have found no examples of L-->I. Similarly, the unattested phrase "Myth is the mother of religion" suggests L-->L.

Certain connections will seem possible to some readers but not others. Can Behavior affect Feeling ("My own screaming made me afraid")? Can Behavior affect Intellect ("Drinking made me stupid")? Can Behavior affect Belief ("Self-sacrifice is the mother of belief")? Can Behavior affect Behavior, as in the attested "Gambling is the father of mischief"? My own personal extension of the model takes none of these as direct links in the model. I take them as one of two things: (1) Concatenations that run through World. Mind may find itself drunk, a physiological situation, which affects its operation. I may think about my behavior as an object to be contemplated, or I may have certain emotional reactions to the fact of my behavior, and this thinking and feeling may in turn result in other feelings, ideas, or beliefs, which in turn may affect my behavior. (2) Direct links, but outside the model. It is possible for the body to affect the body directly: "Falling down the stairs (Behavior) caused my bleeding all over myself (Behavior)." This is causation outside the domain of *lineage*. A phrase like "Running is the mother of good breathing" could, as I take it, be both body affecting itself directly, and a concatenation such as Behavior (running) affects World (the situation of being fit) affects Feeling (being calm) affects Behavior (calm, deep breathing). A behaviorist might make different extensions of the basic model to handle such cases.

A certain set of direct links is forbidden. Mind cannot affect World directly, except in the supernatural. God's wrath can be the father of destruction directly, but mine cannot.

Concatenations. If we look at the extended basic model, we find a cycle $W \rightarrow F \rightarrow B \rightarrow W$. It is a permutation group. I will represent it as (WFB) to indicate that theoretically the generation could loop forever and that one may begin or end at any point. There are also four cycles through F: (FF), (FI), (FL), and (FIL). I will call these F-cycles.

Given any expansion of any cycle, we can substitute for any F in that expansion any F-cycle expansion provided both

(1) the F-cycle expansion has F as terminal node

and

(2) either the replaced F is the initial node, or the F-cycle expansion has F as its initial node.

Let me give an example in plainer English. (WFB) might be expanded to

FBWFBWFBWFBWF

For the first F, we could substitute L→F, an expansion of (FL). For the second, we could substitute F→I→F, an expansion of (FI). For the third, we could substitute F→I→L→F, an expansion of (FIL). For the fourth, we could substitute F→L→F, an expansion of (FL). This would give us

LFBWFIFBWFILFBWFLFBWF

There is a countable infinity of possible concatenations. There is even a countable infinity of concatenations contained within Mind. Perhaps this contributes to our vague and naive sense that influence cascades indefinitely through the world, the mind, and behavior.

Do any of these concatenations occur in the data? Yes. Readers and writers understand how to chain generations to make a path through the model and will often give or expect only the initial and final terms, under the assumption that intermediate links are implicitly indicated by the shared model. For example, the World situation can affect Feeling, and Feeling can lead to Behavior; so the World situation (initial term) can lead to a certain kind of Behavior (final term). Intervening transformations can be omitted; they will be supplied by the understander.

Here are the clear concatenations I have found:

World → Behavior

Poverty is the mother of crimes. (La Bruyère)

The chain is: World situation (poverty) affects Feeling, which generates Behavior (crimes).

So is she that cometh, the mother of songs. (Pound)

The chain is: the woman (World situation) generates a Feeling, which generates production of song (Behavior), which optionally further generates existence of song (World situation).

Necessity is the mother of invention.

The World situation, necessity or lack, leads to a Feeling of need or desire, which induces a certain kind of planning Behavior, involving the invention of things to satisfy the need.

By yawning Sloth on his owne mother Night (Spenser)

Sloth as Feeling and Behavior are not separated.

> I congratulate you on the repeal of that mother of mischief, the Stamp Act. (Franklin, OED)

Here, multiple understandings are possible, because the intermediate generations are omitted. One path is: the Stamp Act (World situation) generates resentment of Stamp Act by Americans (Feeling), which generates mischief by Americans to interfere with the Stamp Act (Behavior).

Feeling → World

> . . . this Man of Clay, Son of despite,
> Whom us the more to spite his Maker rais'd
> From dust (Milton)

The chain is Feeling (despite) affects Behavior (the creation of man), resulting in a new World situation (the existence of man).

Some other concatenations are less clear. Is "harm" Behavior or World situation or even Feeling in "ignourance be mooder of alle harm" (Chaucer)? Clearly it is a concatenation beginning with the Intellect, but we are given some freedom in determining where it stops, which could be a way of indicating that ignorance has a range of effects.

The most controversial plausible concatenations present Behavior as both initial and final term.

Behavior → Behavior

> Gambling is . . . the father of mischief.

> For Commerce, tho the child of Agriculture (Blake)

> Idleness is a mother. She has a son, robbery. (Hugo, trans. Wilbour)

Consider Richard Osborne's statement that Mahler's "First Symphony was the tempestuous child of the union" (i.e. Mahler's love affair with the wife of Weber's grandson). One kind of Behavior (a love affair) induces another kind of Behavior (the writing of a particular tempestuous symphony). Is this link direct or concatenated? I understand the statement as follows: The World situation (the wife, etc.) affects

Mahler's Feeling. This Feeling leads to the Behavior of the love affair. This Behavior alters the World situation, which affects Mahler's Feeling, which leads to the Behavior of writing music.

I noted earlier that Wordsworth's address to Kilchurn castle as "child of loud-throated war" could be B→W. But someone who pushes the understanding further might see it as a concatenation. The castle may be seen as either promoting war or responding to war: the building of the castle can be either belligerent or defensive. In the first case, War (belligerency) results in the existence of the castle directly. In the second, war (belligerency) results in a World situation threatening to others, which induces a Feeling of defensiveness, which leads to the defensive Behavior of building the castle, which leads to the existence of the castle, a change in the World situation.

This illustrates something crucial: *different readers might find different paths through the model of the generations, one path frequently a shortcut of the other; but all readers seek to understand by finding a path through the shared model.* This means that a given example need not correspond to a unique path in the model. Nor need an example correspond to the shortest path through the model. Indeed, we may feel that some looping is done through the model to take us away from and bring us back to some point in it, but not feel that we know how much looping is done, or even what paths the looping may take.

Lateral relations. Lateral relations indicate that two Feelings or Behaviors have the same mental source, or result from the same or very close operations of the mind, or bear some other similarity:

Cant is the twin sister of hypocrisy.

A boaster and a liar are cousins.

Accuracy is the twin brother of honesty.

Ha! ha! what a fool Honesty is! and Trust his sworn brother, a very simple gentleman! (Shakespeare)

(More examples in appendix 2H.)

Occasionally in such cases it is also implied that the two Feelings or Behaviors are concomitant:

Lasciviousnesse is known to be
The sister to saturitie. (Herrick)

After Glotonye thanne comth Lecherie, for these two
synnes been so ny cosyns that often tyme they wol nat
depart. (Chaucer)

2.7 Connotations

In this section, I take up three related topics: (1) how the
connotations of x and y constrain the selection of kinship
terms in kinship metaphors, (2) what connotations each
specific kinship term evokes, and (3) how connotations of
kinship terms constrain the metaphoric inference patterns.

Constraint of kinship term

Often, the connotations of a subject x strongly constrain
the kinship metaphor. For instance, since "moon" connotes
femininity in English, a writer choosing a kinship term as a
metaphor for "moon" must either select a nonmasculine
term or expect his reader to notice that a connotation has
been violated.

The object y can, atypically, constrain the selection of the
kinship term: in "The child is the father of the man," the
referents of subject and object are the same person; hence
the masculinity of "man" transfers to "child," which requires
the kinship term equated with "child" to be masculine.

Just as metaphoric inference patterns can cohere, as discussed in 2.6, so a metaphoric inference pattern can cohere
with *constraint of kinship term*. *Property transfer* frequently
coheres with *constraint of kinship term* when the subject x
suggests but does not require certain connotations. In such a
case, the writer can choose a kinship term that reinforces the
suggestion, thereby combining *constraint* and *property
transfer* simultaneously and reinforcingly.

These two inference patterns can also combine simultaneously in such a way as not to be necessarily reinforcing. Suppose *constraint* requires that the kinship term be not feminine, and *causation* requires that the term denote offspring.
Then, adhering to *constraint*, the writer may choose between
the terms "child" and "son." He may additionally wish to
transfer a connotation of one of the terms but not the other

to the subject, and thus make his selection so as to employ *property transfer*. But the *constraint* and the *property transfer* do not reinforce each other in that case; they have different motivations.

Connotations of kinship terms

All along, it has been clear that understanders of English are expected to be familiar with certain idealized mental models of kinship and individual kinship relations if they are to succeed at understanding kinship metaphors. What are the connotations we have encountered?

First, the kinship term always connotes *biological relation.* Though language can distinguish between biological and social relations (e.g., *genitor* vs. *pater,* or natural father vs. adoptive father); though anthropologists and sociologists may often find their research concentrating on the social family; and though, plausibly, social relations often hold preeminence in conceptual systems, yet in cases of kinship metaphor, biological and social relations are collapsed, under the assumption that prototypically the social relation follows as a consequence of the biological relation. A mother in cases of kinship metaphor is a natural mother, carrying the connotations of the biological relation. Something conflicting with these connotations will be called a "stepmother" explicitly.

The structure of kinship terms as a lexical category, and the mapping of that structure onto genealogical trees, also induce certain connotations. Descriptions of unique kin relations combine, in English, into categories: for example, the father's youngest brother's first son and the mother's oldest brother's last son are both called "cousin." In the immediate family, mother and father remain distinct, a male offspring is reduced to the category "son," a female offspring to "daughter," an offspring to "child," one's parents' male offspring to "brother," and one's parents' female offspring to "sister." So the same kinship term can apply to different members of an immediate family, and this holds throughout one's kinship tree. Additionally, spouses are united into one category if a kinship relation is traced through either of them as an intermediate. Thus your uncle can be any of the brothers of either of your parents. The collapsing of (usually sexually distinguished) offspring and of spouses as intermediary relations might be accounted for by various theories of kinship structure. Here it suffices to observe that, aside from simplifying one's kinship tree and thus bringing more of it within mental grasp, this collapsing categorizes relatives on the basis not only of lineage but also, consequently, of expected behavior. Calling two relatives by the same term signals a similarity in their expected behavior toward the ego of the tree and the expected behavior of that ego toward them. Thus, to the child, both his mother's eldest brother and his father's youngest brother are, in the stereotypical model, to behave toward him similarly and he is to behave similarly toward them; but to his mother, one is her brother and the other her brother-in-law, connoting two dissimilar sets of mutual behaviors. Thus a given term, though applicable to perhaps many people, carries connotations of personal affection, of expected behavior, of rules of behavior, and of rites and duties, or, as an anthropologist might say, of affect, practice, etiquette, and obligation.

The actual relative frequencies of individual kinship metaphors connote their relative degrees of centrality and peripherality. "Mother" and "child" overwhelmingly dominate kinship metaphor. They are clearly the center, followed only at a distance by "father," "daughter," and "son," then by "brother" and "sister." I have found one metaphoric use of a term more than one vertical step away: "x is the grand-daddy of all y," as in "That was the grand-daddy of all hurricanes." This is a case of *property transfer*: grand-daddies in such cases are big or powerful or pure in genetic stock or have been famous a long time or whatever, and they transfer some such property to x. Similarly for "He's the great-grand-daddy of all sea bass." One can also call someone "grandfather" as a term of affection or veneration. This is *functional property transfer*. Terms involving both vertical and lateral steps occur less often—"uncle" and "cousin" being the most frequent. Except for "cousin," the result of three steps—one up, one across, and one down—I have found no metaphorical uses of terms involving more than two steps. "Husband" and "wife" are altogether peripheral. Step-relations, particularly "stepmother" and "stepchild," occupy an isolated

category; they do not cooperate with regular kinship metaphor inference patterns but rather have a unique metaphorical subinference pattern under *functional property transfer.*

Each individual kinship term has connotations, by which I
mean that a speaker of English is expected to be familiar
with certain idealized mental models suggested by each kinship term. (At the risk of stating the obvious, I note here
that anyone offended by prejudices of various sorts implicit
in the English language will have found ample reason to be
appalled at the stereotypical pictures of gender distinctions
and step-relations implicit in our traditions of kinship metaphor.) Throughout cases of kinship metaphor, females are
characterized by the distinction between high and low,
standing for ideals or deviousness, for angels in white or
daughters of the devil. Typically, they are either above
reproach, removed as it were from society, or, if in society,
manipulated and manipulating. Virtue, truth, beauty, purity,
and hope can all be feminine; so can cant, hypocrisy, illusion,
distrust, and weakness. Ideal virtues can be feminine, but
those virtues involving calculation or related to social deal-
ings tend to be masculine. (Infrequently and exceptionally, a
social activity can be a mother.) Note how jarring it is to
read the unattested "Love is the father of purity." Mystical
concepts and systems regarded as having deep, unknowable,
non-reducible inner workings are almost always female rather
than male. There is a connotation of diffusion attached to
female terms: a system with individuated components
operating in an analytically understandable way can be masculine, but when any complicated system is regarded holistically, then it is feminine. A ship, when regarded holistically,
is feminine. Often in cases of kinship metaphor, a female
state generates a male activity. Activity—particularly social
activity—with an individuated agent is masculine, but there
are counterexamples under "mother" since mother has so
many connotations. Pretty and graceful things are feminine.
Strength and power and strong, active evil are typically masculine. Negative qualities that are not active behaviors tend
to be female. Carriers of potential for life are feminine.

Mothers, usually, are diffuse states, conditions, or places
(like desire, love of money, poverty, ignorance, silence, age,

filth, despair, night, England), but there are two examples in which active behaviors might be mothers: "Trade is the mother of money" and "Freight is the mother of wages." Nurturing states must be mothers rather than fathers.

Few concepts qualify to be fathers. "Father" can connote stateliness and abstraction (time can be a father).

"Child" carries by far the most stereotypical connotations. A child can be, in various idealized mental models, the loved result of labor, an object of education and enculturation, a developing and malleable thing, a caused thing. It contains and summarizes, in miniature, its parents. A child is ignorant, untutored, as yet lacking sufficient experience to understand its existence. It is wise because its insight is not yet clouded by socialization. It is innocent, sweet, winsome. It is both childish and childlike in its emotional patterns: unserious, playful, frisky, joyful, mischievous, mirthful. It connotes naturalness and rebirth. It has rights by inheritance. It inherits beliefs, and hence "children" can mean "lesser cohorts" as in "children of the devil." Many of these connotations combine to connote submissiveness.

"Daughter" has the strongest connotation of submissiveness and dependency, of passivity and inaction; she is not an individuated socially active agent. A daughter is an object of wooing. She is stereotypically graceful and beautiful.

"Son" can have strong connotations of activity and inheritance.

"Brother" can connote activity and strength. When beliefs are shared, it is brothers who share them, though that is changing. Sisterhood is becoming more powerful.

"Twin" intensifies closeness and removes the stereotypical connotations of opposition between siblings. It can connote close companionship, or identity save on unimportant details, or that two concepts are the same essence in two different avatars, especially the same trait in two different manifestations.

There are more and less sophisticated uses of kinship terms. "Brother" or "sister," for instance, can be used merely to indicate similarity, with no careful attention to their connotations. Thus the kinship term can be used decoratively or thoughtlessly.

Constraint of metaphoric functions by kinship connotations

These connotations of course constrain all metaphoric use of kinship terms. Our representation of any concept limits, constrains, motivates, and guides its metaphoric uses. We could not have an *inheritance* inference pattern if kinship could not carry connotations of inheritance.

These connotations also constrain the particular inner mechanics of each inference pattern. For example, a step-relation can be used to indicate that a certain thing ignores, neglects, dismisses, or diminishes another thing, often by refusing to acknowledge its rights, as in "The navy has been the stepchild of both parliaments." But we nonetheless cannot say "Joy is the stepmother of anxiety," or "Domestic energy is the stepmother of OPEC," or "Trade embargo is the stepmother of foreign import profiteering," or "Blinding pain is the stepmother of casual neurosis" because these violate either the negative connotations of *stepparent* or the connotation of sympathy for a *child in the care of a stepparent.*

2.8 Case studies

For simplicity of presentation, I offered in section 2.6 the metaphoric inferences one at a time, with analysis and examples. This violated the complexity of any given example, because many metaphoric inferences and idealized mental models may interact in a single kinship metaphor. Here I repair that violation by analyzing particular cases one at a time.

1. "Babylon is the mother of harlots and abominations."

This combines (1) *place and time as parent*, (2) *property transfer*, (3) *inheritance*, (4) *causation*, and (5) *biological resource as parent.*

A *place and time* location can give birth to occupants and *treat* them as a parent might treat a child: it educates them, rewards and punishes them, provides resources and guidance, requires adherence to certain pieties and regimens. The object must be capable of being personified and of developing under or responding to a stereotypically parental treatment. Here, Babylon generates occupants and raises them according to its principles.

Raising something can imply bequest of principles, hence *inheritance*, particularly *inheritance* of Beliefs. The harlots and practitioners of abomination have *inherited* their nefarious practices from Babylon. Leading something to become what it is by nurturing parentally is also *causation as progeneration*.

Since the necessities—parents, food, air, and so on—for the *biological resource as parent* and physiological maturing of the harlots are in Babylon, Babylon can be the biological mother of the harlots (though not of the abominations), just as the Earth is our mother biologically.

Property transfer coheres with all these inference patterns since ascribing parental behavior to Babylon is *property transfer*. More specifically, *property transfer* characterizes Babylon as motherly, partially because biological generation and nurturing are, in kinship metaphor, motherly, though fathers can bequeath beliefs. Indeed, where the beliefs or principles are abstract and rational, particularly in cases of philosophy and politics, mothers are not mentioned.

Feminizing Babylon follows the tradition of feminizing cities, countries, ships, automobiles, and so on (e.g., "and the little ship is there; yet she is gone," from Lawrence's "The Ship of Death"). Kinship metaphor helps explain this tradition. There are, it seems, three ways to model physical systems conceptually: (1) in terms of physics, as for electrical circuits; (2) in terms of components and their combined operations, as for stereo systems; and (3) anthropomorphically, as for intelligent machines, countries, and so on. In the third case, personifying something leads us to understand it in terms of its purposes, goals, desires, and intentions. But when this calculus of human intention and decision does not work, does not predict the system, when the system is too complex, or when we can ascribe to the system human traits but no particular motivation for having them—in sum, when the system behaves more like a human than like a consistent and reduced model of a human, then personification almost always feminizes the system. This fits connotations given to femininity of mysteriousness, of deep, unknowable, nonreducible inner workings, of holistic and emergent properties, of alternatives to the calculus of rationality. Whatever the anthropology behind these connotations, from the biological marvel of birth to the role of women in religions, kinship metaphor reflects it consistently.

2. "By yawning Sloth on his owne mother Night"

This combines (1) *lineage*, (2) *place and time as parent*, and (3) *constraint*.

Place and time as parent turns Sloth, often concomitant with night, into night's child. Because sloth and night are world-mind-behavior terms, *lineage* operates to specify that sloth not only occurs during night but also is induced by night. The underlying path of generation is World (night) affects Feeling, which in turn leads to the specified Behavior (sloth). Night as soporific generates somnolence, torpidity, sloth. Since night—with its connotations of mysteriousness, irrationality, lunar light, hidden realities—is overwhelmingly feminized in English (as is the moon), the kinship term is *constrained* to be feminine.

3. "The moon is the mother of pathos and pity."

This combines (1) *lineage*, (2) *place and time as parent*, and (3) *constraint*.

Lineage indicates that the presence of the moon (a World situation) generates pathos and pity (Feelings). Since the moon implies—conceptually if not in fact—night, *place and time as parent* also operates: night generates the emotions typical of its duration.

The statement could mean that one of the various emotions which the moon symbolizes—from feminine softness to terror and the irrational—makes pathos and pity possible, induces in us a sympathy. The moon, the night, Dionysian communion, self-transcendence, and the loss of distinct self-individuation can all appear naturally to suggest pathos and pity, in a way sunlight and noontime cannot. The femininity of the kinship term may result from *constraint* exerted by these connotations.

4. "Ignorance is the mother of suspicion."

This combines (1) *causation*, (2) *lineage*, (3) *property transfer*, and (4) *constraint*.

Since "ignorance" and "suspicion" are world-mind-behavior terms, the *lineage* inference specifies the *causation*: here, the underlying path is from Intellect (ignorance) to Belief (suspicion).

This statement exemplifies the harmonious and balanced combination of *property transfer* with *constraint* of the kinship term by the subject. Since the unattested "Ignorance is the father of suspicion" would grate against the connotations of "father" usually found in kinship metaphor, it could be argued that "ignorance" *constrains* the kinship term to femininity. Yet since the unattested statement is not an outright violation like the unattested "The moon is the father of pity," it can be argued that feminizing "ignorance" is *property transfer*. This then is a case of the simultaneous and mutually reinforcing coherence of *constraint* and *property transfer*, discussed in section 2.2. Negative qualities that are not active behaviors incline to be feminine in kinship metaphor, and a state or condition is a mother rather than a father.

5. "Necessity is the mother of invention."

This combines (1) *causation* and (2) *lineage*.

"Necessity" could mean inevitability, as in Shelley's "Necessity! thou mother of the world!"* But "invention" implies human behavior, particularly human spontaneity and will. Since inevitability and will conflict, the reader takes "necessity" to mean "need perceived by a person." Since "need" then describes a World situation, the two terms become world-mind-behavior terms and *lineage* provides a path for the *causation*. The underlying path is World situa-

---

*Such a case, like "Hope the best, but hold the Present / Fatal daughter of the Past," derives from a combination of NECESSITY IS CAUSATION and CAUSATION IS PROGENERATION to produce NECESSITY IS PROGENERATION. The understanding of necessity as causation underlies a wide range of common expressions. If we have one thing and another thing it is *necessary that* we have two things; if time passes, it is *necessary that* people age; words are *necessary for* the construction of sentences; an arrow may be *necessary for* a certain event of death; ideas may be *necessary for* progress. We can express these necessities as causations, as in "One and one *make* two," "The passage of time *makes* people old," "Words *make* sentences," "Ideas *bring about* progress," and "The arrow *killed* him."

tion (need) affects Feeling (perception of need) which prompts a goal-based Behavior (invention).

6. "A proverb is the child of experience."

This combines (1) *causation*, (2) *lineage*, and (3) *property transfer*.

For any statement "x is the child of y" where neither x nor y is a person, "child" means "result" under *causation as progeneration*. But since "proverb" and "experience" refer to world-mind-behavior, *lineage* specifies the kind of *causation*. The chain is: World situations (experience) can change Knowledge and Feeling over the long term, which in turn affect Beliefs. Knowledge and Beliefs, through Intellect and Feeling, can lead to Behavior, such as linguistic expression (proverb). The path of generation could be stopped there, or optionally carried a step further: this Behavior results in the existence of a proverb (a change in the World situation).

Note that *causation* here is efficacy, not necessary and sufficient conditions or regularity. It is not that the cause will always produce the effect, or that the cause is necessary or sufficient to produce the effect, or that the cause logically or actually entails the effect, or that nothing else can produce the effect, or that the same cause cannot have different effects, or even that the cause must regularly have the effect. Rather, the cause is seen as having had, at least once, the latent power to produce the effect, and perhaps as retaining that power. A chain of efficacy connects "experience" to "proverb," but that does not imply that other conditions are not important in the chain.

The combining of *causation* and *lineage* specifies the type of efficacy. We know the statement does not mean, for example, that experience sits down and writes a proverb, because *lineage* disallows it.

Property transfer transfers two connotations from "child" to "proverb." First, people struggle to reach a position enabling them to bear and raise children, and they love their children, at least stereotypically. Their love is often all the deeper and more poignant for the struggle of attaining maturity and the woes of child-bearing. In the same way, people love their proverbs or aphorisms; these things are born of them, and their experience makes the birth possible. By analogy, a careful linguistic statement can be seen as a child. Second, children contain and summarize, in miniature, their parents. Generations are a living anaphora. As the parents hand on their knowledge to the child—often by the use of proverbs and similar summaries—so experience hands on its knowledge, in condensed form, to the proverb.

7. "O language, mother of thought"

This combines (1) *causation*, (2) *lineage*, (3) *property transfer*.

The previous example, "A proverb is the child of experience," relied for its understanding upon the common idealized mental model, implicit in the *lineage* model, that the mind produces language (Behavior). The present example illustrates how, to understand a metaphor, we often must revise concepts. It also lets me introduce a claim I argue in the next chapter—that understanding novel or extended kinship metaphor still depends upon locating familiar metaphoric inferences.

As in the last example, *causation as progeneration* applies: thought is the result of language. *Lineage* is called upon to specify the path. For those already familiar, say from Whorf or phrases like "mother tongue," with the general notion that what you can think is somehow constrained by the possibilities of the languages you have learned and that your thought inherits structures from your language, there will be no difficulty in finding the path: repeated interaction with the World (language) affects various components of Mind. But suppose the understander lacks this notion. He will expect from the common model implicit in *lineage* that the Mind produces language (Behavior), not the reverse. Searching for a path in the *lineage* model that can accommodate thought as resulting from language must lead to one of two choices: (1) The perception of a bit of language (say someone speaking a sentence to you) can prompt a thought. This is World situation affects Intellect, which may then affect Belief or Feeling. (2) One's developmental training in language can affect cognition. This is accumulated experience with the World affecting Mind. If the understander selects the second choice, then the metaphor has successfully required him to reconceive or deepen his model of how experience affects the mind. He might be helped in this by other models and conceptual structures he already holds—such as that what one learns at one's mother's breast abides deeply and powerfully in the mind and that mothers teach their infants language.

The context—the following passage from Denise Levertov's "Interim"—will drive the understander to the second choice:

> And,
> "'It became necessary
> to destroy the town to save it,'
> a United States major said today.
> He was talking about the decision
> by allied commanders to bomb and shell the town
> regardless of civilian casualties,
> to rout the Vietcong."
>
> O language, mother of thought,
> are you rejecting us as we reject you?

Functional property transfer characterizes language as motherly: though mothers can nurture and instruct lovingly, they can also reject older children who have disregarded that instruction and love, who have violated or profaned what the mother holds dear.

8. "He was the child of all the dale—he lived / Three months with one, and six months with another."

This combines (1) *place and time as parent*, (2) *biological resource as parent*, (3) *inheritance*, and (4) *property transfer*.

This tight coherence of several major inferences explains the popularity, aptness, and frequency of constructions like "child of Nature," "Nature's child," "child of earth and sky."

Place and time as parent characterizes the occupant of the dale as the offspring of the dale. *Biological resource as parent* makes the recipient of the dale's biological nurturing the progeny of the dale. The dale also *treats* the subject as its dependent.

The salient characteristics of the dale—its rusticity and naturalness—are *inherited* by the kinship term and then transferred to the subject. As a consequence, he is characterized as rustic and natural. The subject *behaves-as* a child (in one stereotype) behaves; that is, he behaves naturally and without sophistication.

9. "And wooed the artless daughter of the hills."

This combines (1) *place and time as parent*, (2) *inheritance*, (3) *property transfer*, and (4) *lineage*.

This repeats the combination in "He was the child of all the dale," also Wordsworth's, above. "Artless" reinforces the *inheritance* of the naturalness and rusticity of the hills. That a girl is the subject, and a girl to be wooed at that, *constrains* the kinship term to femininity.

10. "You are the child of the universe. You have a right to be here."

This combines (1) *place and time as parent*, (2) *biological resource as parent*, (3) *property transfer*, and (4) *inheritance*.

The occupant of the universe is, by *place and time as parent*, its offspring, and, by *biological resource as parent*, its biological progeny. *Treated-as*, a subcategory of *functional property transfer*, implies that the subject is both nurtured and loved by the universe.

Property transfer, prompted by the explanatory pointer after the statement, transfers to "you" a child's rights of existence and its privilege to be nurtured by what produced it, regardless of its own contribution to its existence.

The highlight of the statement is *inheritance*: as a child of the universe, you inherit its patterns and essence and hence necessarily harmonize with it. This typifies the frequent strong coherence between *place and time as parent* and *inheritance*.

11. "Gambling is the child of avarice, the brother of iniquity, the father of mischief."

This combines (1) *causation* and (2) *lineage*; then (1) *group*, (2) *lineage*, and (3) *property transfer*; then (1) *causation*, (2) *lineage*, and (3) *property transfer*.

Since "gambling," "avarice," "iniquity," and "mischief" are world-mind-behavior terms, *lineage* operates throughout: in the first case, it indicates a path of generation from Feeling (avarice) to Behavior (gambling); in the second, it indicates that gambling and iniquity are concomitant behaviors sharing a mental source; in the third, it indicates a (perhaps concatenated) path of generation from Behavior (gambling) to Behavior (mischief).

Gambling, an activity, and particularly a social activity dominated by men, is therefore made masculine by *property transfer*.

12. "Sleep is the brother of death." "There was peace after death, the brother of sleep." "Death is the mother of beauty." "Sleep, Death's twin brother." "Night, sister of heavy death."

The first two combine (1) *similarity* and (2) *property transfer*. Note that only real-world knowledge can indicate which of three inferences operates: (1) *group*—meaning that sleep and death are companions; (2) *lineage*—meaning that sleep and death are (perhaps concomitant) behaviors with the same mental source; or (3) *similarity*. Only the reader's real-world knowledge can reject the first two.

Kinship metaphor in the West—with the exception of a small subgenre in which death is a seductive mistress—makes death masculine since feminine terms strongly connote life and potential for life. Examples are:

> Death with most grim and griesly visage seen,
> Yet is he nought but parting of the breath. (Spenser)

> Lo! Death has reared himself a throne
> In a strange city lying alone
> Far down within the dim West (Poe)

> Because I could not stop for Death—
> He kindly stopped for me— (Dickinson)

Wallace Stevens adheres to the expectation in "There was peace after death, the brother of sleep" but violates it in the startlingly atypical "Death is the mother of beauty." This violation illuminates subtleties of *property transfer*. The poet's use of the feminine rather than the masculine kinship term robs death of some of its usual connotations and requires a conceptual revision. The generation is benign; the production of beauty is nurtured maternally; and death is connected with beauty, which is always feminine. The triply strange rebellion of this statement from usual usage—making death a generator, a female, and the parent of beauty—

manipulates the reader into understanding "death" as "the perception of death." How does this happen? A mother progenerates life, but death is the opposite of progeneration. How can this conflict be resolved? If "death" is taken to mean "the perception by someone of death," or, metaphorically, of cessation and loss, then *lineage* can operate, and death, as an observed phenomenon, can progenerate the perception of beauty.

Tennyson atypically (for English) calls death and sleep twin brothers, raising two points. When a writer uses a kinship term that violates expectations, the reader must presuppose, to understand it, either that the deviation is conscious and meaningful—as in "Death is the mother of beauty"—or that the writer's language and concepts differ from the reader's own. In cases of English kinship metaphor, twinship indicates close companionship ("We are twin brothers in this destiny") or identity save on unimportant details ("Heere's the twyn-brother of thy Letter" where the letters differ only in address) or that the two concepts are the same essence in two different avatars, especially the same trait in two different manifestations. (Examples are "Twin Sisters still were ignorance and pride," "False Shame discarded, spurious Fame despised, Twin Sisters both of Ignorance," "Humility, with its twin sister meekness," "Prejudice is the twin of illiberality." A particular shape takes two manifestations in "A boat twin-sister of the crescent moon" and art takes two forms in "Music is twin-sister to poetry," where *group* also operates.) The reader can understand the twin relation of death and sleep by assuming either that the poet does not understand the usual connotations of "twin brother" and that he means "brother," or that the poet has some reason for perceiving death and sleep as much closer than usual. The second is in fact the case:

> When in the down I sink my head,
>   Sleep, Death's twin brother, times my breath;
>   Sleep, Death's twin brother, knows not Death;
> Nor can I dream of thee as dead. (Tennyson)

Sleep in these lines from *In Memoriam* is seen as a kind of replacement for death, as comparable in power to death since it can undo the effects of death.

Hesiod's *Theogony* (212) calls Sleep and Death, brothers, the offspring of Night (Νὺξ δ' ἔτεκεν στυγερόν τε Μόρον καὶ Κῆρα μέλαιναν / καὶ Θάνατον, τέκε δ' Ὕπνον). In Homer's *Iliad* (16.672 and 682), Sleep and Death are called twin brothers (Ὕπνῳ καὶ Θανάτῳ διδυμάοσιν). Consequently, Scott and Liddel's *Greek-English Lexicon* lists Sleep and Death as twin brothers.

In "Night, sister of heavy Death" (Spenser), night, with strong connotations of femininity, is *constrained* to be a sister. The question, indeed, is why sleep is constrained in the above examples to be masculine. The power of sleep to conquer, to overpower us, even against our most resolved will, and by sheer manifest advance rather than subterfuge or seduction, may account for its gender here.

13.   "Ah, brother of the brief but blazing star!
　　　 What hast thou to do with these
　　　 Haunting the bank's historic trees?
　　　 Thou born for noblest life,
　　　 For action's field, for victor's car?" (Emerson)

This example from "In Memoriam E.B.E." combines (1) *similarity* and (2) *constraint*.

That the kinship term stands for E. B. Emerson *constrains* it to be masculine. The specific point of *similarity* between E. B. Emerson and the star is the possession of a brief, blazing life, suggesting a shooting star.

14. "Admiration is the daughter of ignorance." "There is an admiration which is the daughter of knowledge."

These combine (1) *lineage*, (2) *inheritance*, and (3) *property transfer*.

In both cases, the underlying path of generation is Intellect (knowledge, ignorance) affects Beliefs (admiration). And in both cases, the kinship term *inherits* the salient characteristic of the object (ignorance, knowledge) and transfers it to the subject (admiration). One kind of admiration derives from ignorance since knowledge would eliminate it.

Property transfer characterizes admiration as daughter-like, submissive and dependent. The feminizing of admiration may be consonant with a stereotype of women as supportive and even doting, as looking up to men, standing behind them and encouraging them.

15. "Hope the best, but hold the Present / Fatal daughter of the Past."

This combines (1) *causation* and (2) *property transfer.*

This is a rare example of kinship metaphor that might be taken as suggesting determinism, but the suggestion is both vague and forced. Kinship metaphor does not naturally connote fatalism; no component of daughterhood suggests inevitability. Fated occurrence must be pushed into the metaphor by the adjective "fatal." "Daughter" implies consequence, and "fatal" perhaps implies fated consequence, but their conjunction violates the concept of *causation as progeneration* inherent in the metaphor and upheld throughout the genre. This violation seems without purpose—unlike that in the triply strange "Death is the mother of beauty." *Daughter* is stereotypically more submissive than *son*. *Property transfer* thus characterizes the Present as submissive. A "fatal daughter" might in some vague way be thought to be even more submissive, more apt to take on the coloring of a parent. Perhaps Tennyson conceived this rare construction under the influence more of academic philosophy than of traditional English usage.

By calling this construction "rare," I mean not that it is hard to understand, or poetically weak, or unnatural if one has adopted a perspective on time quite frequent in philosophical works, but rather that it is statistically very infrequent and that it conflicts with standard connotations in the rest of the genre.

16. "Stern daughter of the voice of God! O Duty!"

This combines (1) *inheritance* and (2) *property transfer.*

"Daughter" *inherits* the authoritative command of the voice of God and transfers it to duty as a governing characteristic. Duty is feminized by *property transfer*, perhaps because ideal virtues, as opposed to social virtues, are usually feminine in kinship metaphor (though duty is not so clearly feminine as purity), perhaps because the submission of an echo fits daughterhood. But "daughter" and "duty" conflict in their connotations, resulting in the poet's attempt to specify duty as a "stern" daughter, thereby removing various unsuiting connotations of "daughter," such as softness and passivity, from the comparison.

17. "Those were the Graces, daughters of delight."

This combines (1) *inheritance*, (2) *property transfer*, (3) *group*, and (4) *similarity*.

The kinship term *inherits* delight and transfers it to the Graces, further described by the *transfer* to them of femininity, gracefulness, and beauty as properties of "daughter." The Graces are *grouped* by the plural kinship term. Their common parent makes them sisters, *similar* by common *inheritance*.

18. "Tis contemplation, daughter of the grey morning."

This combines (1) *causation*, (2) *lineage*, (3) *place and time as parent*, (4) *inheritance*, and (5) *property transfer*.

Since "grey morning" and "contemplation" are world-mind-behavior terms, *lineage* specifies the path of generation as World situation (grey morning) affects Feeling and perhaps Intellect (contemplation). *Place and time as parent* makes the occupant of grey morning its offspring. Daughter *inherits* connotations of greyness—subdued, unspritely, half-dark—and those connotations of morning not inconsistent with greyness—calm, lassitudinous, half-awake. Passivity, stereotypically possible as a connotation of daughter but not, unless added by some extrinsic semantic operation, of son, is a *property transferred* to contemplation.

19.   "Whispered the Muse in Saadi's cot:
      O gentle Saadi, listen not,
      Tempted by thy praise of wit,
      Or by thirst and appetite
      For the talents not thine own,
      To sons of contradiction.
      Never, son of eastern morning,
      Follow falsehood, follow scorning."

"Sons of contradiction" combines (1) *inheritance*, (2) *property transfer*, (3) *group*, and (4) *similarity*. "Sons" *inherit* the penchant for dispute. *Property transfer* characterizes them as masculine, a stereotypical connotation of intellectual dispute. The plural form *groups* them. They are *similar* in all *inheriting* the same characteristic.

"Son of eastern morning" combines (1) *place and time as parent*, (2) *biological resource as parent*, and (3) *inheritance*. The masculine subject *constrains* the kinship term to masculinity. Eastern morning produced Saadi under both *place and time as parent* and, since the East biologically produced and nurtured him, *biological resource as parent*. "Son" *inherits* some connotations of Eastern morning—particularly the intellectual and behavioral connotations of the East—and transfers them to Saadi. The context assists the determination of which connotations are inherited, that is, those opposing the Western adversary system and its presupposition of dualities like truth and falsehood and its two further presuppositions that words are fit captors of ideas and that reason is the ultimate tribunal of truth.

20. "Cant is the twin sister of hypocrisy." "Accuracy is the twin brother of honesty."

Both cases combine (1) *similarity*, (2) *lineage*, and (3) *property transfer*.

Property transfer characterizes cant and hypocrisy as feminine, and honesty and accuracy as masculine.

"Twin sister" and "twin brother" primarily indicate *similarity*. But since "cant," "hypocrisy," "accuracy," and "honesty" refer to behavior, *lineage* gives a more specific, coherent indication that in each pair the two behaviors have the same mental source; they result from the same or very close operations of the mind. Therein lies the *similarity*.

To be sure, context might compel the reader to understand these examples as indicating concomitancy, as in "How do you know he is honest?" "Well, I have observed that he is an accurate man—accurate even in minute things, accurate even when he is ignorant of my scrutiny—; and accuracy is the twin brother of honesty." But this understanding is forced.

Rather, "twin sister" and "twin brother" imply that the two components spring from the same underlying component of personality. "Twin" always intensifies closeness, but here it has other, related properties. Identical twins have identical origins, not just, as in the case of nontwin brothers and sisters, common parents. Thus "brother" and "sister," though indicating similarity, also connote sibling rivalry, jealousy, difference, sometimes opposition. Folk tales often pit the good brother against the bad, the white witch against her dark sister, as if their powers—similar and cognate—have taken different surface level shapes, have assumed different avatars. "Twin" removes these oppositions. Thus, a reader will understand "Truth is the sister of beauty" because it leaves room for conflict. But he will likely understand "Truth is the twin sister of beauty" as signaling that the writer has shallow and naive concepts of truth and beauty.

Incidentally, note the role of pragmatics in this case. We have metaphorical meanings for "sister" and "twin sister": the first is to be used for cognate concepts with a sisterlike mix of similarities and oppositions, the other when this mix is absent or insignificant. If an author asserts a kinship relation between two concepts and we have difficulty believing that assertion, we assume that the author's representations of the two concepts differ from ours in precisely this way: he lacks the conflict between the two concepts that prevents us from applying "twin." For "Truth is the twin sister of beauty," we assume that the author's concept of truth includes only simple, comprehensible, Platonic truth and not detailed and unmanageable truth; that his concept of beauty is equally Platonic, lacking representations of beauty as delusion or illusion or artifice. *Knowledge about the author influences our processes of understanding.* A writer we regard as particularly shallow and who says "Beauty is Truth" will be understood as having representations of truth and beauty sufficiently shallow to permit his matching them. A Keats saying "Beauty is Truth" may be honored with the benefit of the doubt: we may suspect him of having representations of truth and beauty sufficiently profound to permit his locating an overwhelming deep equality between two concepts that, for us, have surface conflicts.

APPENDIX

Appendix 2A: Step-relations

Negligence is stepdame of lernynge. (OED)

The world hath been a step-dame to me. (OED)

He seem'd to carry Reason along with him, who called Nature Step-mother, in that she gives us so small a portion of time. (OED)

Fortune to one is a mother, to another is a step-mother. (OED)

Turn'd naked into a frowning step-mother world. (OED)

Poverty is the step-mother of genius.

Appendix 2B: Specified similarity

If carnall Death (the younger brother) doe / Usurpe the body, our soule, which subject is / To th'elder death, by sinne, is freed by this. (Donne)

Hawthorn Hall was not first cousin to the Aspens, having nothing of the villa about it. (Lloyd, OED)

Science, and her sister Poesy, Shall clothe in light the cities of the free! (Shelley, OED)

America, thou half-brother of the world; With something good or bad of every land (Philip James Bailey)

Dieu a fait de moi le frère de Job, / en m'enlevant brutalement / tout ce que j'avais. (Dufournet, trans. Rutebeuf)

Appendix 2C: Unspecified Similarity

Sleep, Death's twin brother (Tennyson)

There should you behold a Mine of Tynne (sister to Silver). (Dekker, OED)

A boat twin-sister of the crescent moon (Wordsworth, OED) (In this case, perhaps "crescent" as shape specifies the similarity.)

Music is twin-sister to poetry. (Horder, OED)

Sleep is the brother of death.

I am the little woodlark.
The skylark is my cousin and he
Is known to men more than me. (Hopkins)

Sith thow hast lernyd by the sentence of Plato that nedes the
wordis moot be cosynes to the thinges of whiche thei speken
(Chaucer)

Appendix 2D: Group

The two renowned and most hopefull Sisters, Virginia and
the Summer-Islands (OED)

Mt. Olivet overtopping its sister, Mt. Moriah, three hundred
feet (OED)

Inspiration decidedly the sister of daily labor (OED)

You did not desert me, my brothers in arms. (Dire Straits)

Appendix 2E: Inheritance

The public child of earth and sky (Emerson)

Of Nature's child the common fate (Emerson)

Those were the Graces, daughters of delight. (Spenser)

Born a poor young country boy / Mother Nature's son (The
Beatles)

Come to me . . . not as . . . a sweet and winsome child of
innocence. (Lawrence)

O thou poor human form
O thou poor child of woe (Blake)

Why weepest thou, Tharmas, child of tears in the bright
house of joy (Blake)

And wooed the artless daughter of the hills (Wordsworth)

Paulus Maximus . . . Child of a hundred Arts (Jonson)

Tis contemplation, daughter of the grey morning. (Blake)

Like to like shall joyful prove
He shall be happy whilst he wooes,
Muse-born, a daughter of the muse. (Emerson)

O darling Katie Willows, his one child!
A maiden of our century, yet most meek;
A daughter of our meadows, yet not coarse (Tennyson)

Among the shepherd-grooms no mate
Hath he, a child of strength and state. (Wordsworth)

Sweetest Shakespeare, Fancy's Child (Milton, OED)

And pray that never child of song
May know that Poet's sorrows more. (Wordsworth)

Thou Child of Joy (Wordsworth)

The meek, the lowly, patient child of toil (Wordsworth)

Now is Cupid a child of conscience; he makes restitution. (Shakespeare)

This child of fancy that Armado hight (Shakespeare)

This same child of honour and renown, This gallant Hotspur (Shakespeare)

Horrid night, the child of hell (Shakespeare)

Light (God's eldest daughter) is a principal beauty in building. (Thomas Fuller)

Midonz, daughter of the sun, shaft of the tree, silver of the leaf, light of the yellow of the amber (Pound)

That great child of Honor, Cardinal Wolsey (Shakespeare)

The daughter of debate, that eke discord doth sow [said of Mary Queen of Scots] (Queen Elizabeth I)

We love not this French God, the child of Hell,
Wild War, who breaks the converse of the wise. (Tennyson)

O Chatterton! . . . Dear child of sorrow—son of misery! (Keats)

The child of genius sits forlorn. (Emerson)

But, for that moping Son of Idleness (Wordsworth)

the sonnes of darknes and of ignoraunce (Spenser)

The fierce Croation, and the wild Hussar
And all the sons of ravage croud the war (Jonson)

Forther ouer, it makyth hym that whilom was a son of Ire to be a son of Grace (Chaucer, OED)

That bronzeshod spear this child of Power [Athena] can use
/ to break in wrath long battlelines of fighters. (*Odyssey*

1.101, trans. Fitzgerald. ὀβριμοπάτρη = daughter of a powerful father, used again as an epithet for Athena at *Iliad* 5.747).

O Day Star, son of Dawn [said of Lucifer] (Isa. 14:12-14)

Son of perdition [what the friar calls the fool who has insulted him] (More, trans. Adams)

I've been searchin' for the daughter of the devil himself. (The Eagles)

Sons of Morn [said of angels] (Milton)

Locks of auburn, and eyes of blue, have ever been dear to the sons of song. (Strangford, OED)

Italian, eldest daughter of ancient Latin

Appendix 2F: Inherited beliefs

Thomas Carlyle . . . is in spirit a child of the great revolution. (Harrison, OED)

We are today living with a faith, an aspiration that, rooted though it is in several thousand years of Western history, is still, in the forms we must live with, the child of the Age of Reason. (Crane Brinton)

Kant, Immanuel: German metaphysician and moralist, a good child of the Age of Reason whose reputation actually increased in the Romantic Age. (Crane Brinton)

Appendix 2G: Inheritance of both characteristics and beliefs

Stern daughter of the voice of God! O Duty! (Wordsworth)

We be all good English men. Let us bang these dogs of Seville, the children of the devil, For I never turned my back upon Don or devil yet. (Tennyson)

Some folks inherit star-spangled eyes / Ooh, they send you down to war. / And when you ask them, 'How much should we give?' / They only answer 'More, more, more.' / It ain't me. / It ain't me. / I ain't no military son. (Creedence Clearwater Revival)

The brightest Angell, even the Child of Light (Spenser)

Angels Progeny of Light (Milton)

Ethereal sons [of Heaven] [said of angels] (Milton)

Sons of Heaven [said of angels] (Milton)

Venice, the eldest Child of Liberty (Wordsworth)

Appendix 2H: Lateral Relations

Humility, with its twin sister meekness (Norris, OED)

The Sophist is the cousin of the parasite and the flatterer. (Plato, trans. Jowett, OED)

Twin Sisters still were Ignorance and Pride. (Prior, OED)

In vain [I] am driven on false hope, hope sister of despair. (Blake)

Her former sorrow into suddein wrath,
Both cousin passions of distroubled spright (Spenser)

Prejudice is the twin of illiberality.

Vayne glory, with her other sisters, inobedience, boasting, etc. (OED)

3 *Literary Texts*

I have demonstrated so far how a few basic metaphors, metaphoric inference patterns, and idealized cognitive models can underlie a wide range of utterances. I now want to extend that demonstration to a wide range of literary texts. We seek to understand an extended simile based on kinship metaphor exactly as we seek to understand the kinship metaphors we have already seen, by locating the metaphoric inference patterns of the kinship terms. This implies that we generally understand similes as extended conceptual metaphors. Concretely, in this chapter I demonstrate how certain texts depend upon metaphoric inferences like *inheritance*, *place and time as parent*, and *causation*.

The selection of texts here is meant to be illustrative merely. Other texts might have been chosen that would have served the demonstration equally well. I am concerned not so much to analyze the contributions of kinship metaphors within the particular texts as to discuss how these metaphoric patterns transcend their individual functions within particular texts and consequently belong to a pattern in the high canon of Western literature. I discuss a quasi-religious text like Hesiod's *Theogony* in the same context with fictions like *The Faerie Queene* because common cognitive processes underlie kinship metaphor wherever it appears. For the same reason, I sprinkle together good poetry and bad. What cognitive apparatus underlies bland and flat texts is a tough and fertile question. In speaking of Milton and

Blake in the same breath with Martianus Capella, I do not intend to reduce Milton and Blake. On the contrary, when we understand what is common to our languages, we may understand why a particular use of these commonalities strikes us as compelling. The common is the foil for the superior. We see genius in art not at all for inexplicable, mystical reasons but rather when we behold artists using processes masterfully, perhaps dovetailing many meanings and effects coherently, reinforcingly, and compendiously.

The texts we will look at fall into two natural categories by subject matter. Some concern the *human condition*, others the *cosmos*, and I will follow this division, because the texts in each category often relate tightly. But I break this organization by subject matter in one case: though usually marriage is a metaphor for progenerative coupling, some texts employ marriage as a metaphor for *union and blending*, and these texts I treat in a separate, third category.

The texts are: (1) *human condition* texts: Milton's Satan-Sin-Death episode in *Paradise Lost,* Gower's Satan-Sin-Death-Seven Vices episodes in *Mirour de l'omme*, God's curse on the serpent, on Eve, and on Adam in Genesis 3, Blake's elaborate genealogy of components of human psychology in "then She bore Pale desire," and passages from Spenser's *Faerie Queene* concerning psychology and behavior; (2) *cosmos* texts: Hesiod's *Theogony*, against a background of ancient Near Eastern and Roman cosmogonies, and Milton's, Spenser's, and Gower's various genealogies of Chaos and Nothingness; (3) *marriage as union and blending* texts: John Redford's *Wit and Science* and Martianus Capella's *De Nuptiis Philologiae et Mercurii.*

Human condition: Satan, Sin, and Death in Milton

Lines 648-849 of book 2 of *Paradise Lost* depict Satan, aflame with arrogance and evil design, encountering but not recognizing Sin and Death at the gates of Hell, out of which he expects, no mistake, to exit. When Death obstructs his progress, they volley infernal insults and threats, but Sin's call halts their imminent violence. They converse, and though the Almighty has bidden Sin and Death to guard the locked gates, Satan, with liquid oratory and the deceit of gorgeous rhetoric, allies Sin and Death to him by alleging common interests, just as he will later beguile the forces of Chaos and Night. In this exchange, Sin reveals that she is Satan's daughter, upon whom Satan has incestuously begotten a son, Death. Death in turn has begotten incestuously upon Sin a pack of yelling monsters. (Cf. James 1:15, "Then when lust hath conceived, it bringeth forth sin; and Sin, when it is finished, bringeth forth death.") The Satan-Sin-Death episode reveals paradigmatically the fundamental problem of metaphor in literature: one thing, kinship, both matches and does not match with another thing, in this case the system of relationships between Satan, Sin, and Death. The poet draws on those points of similarity and relies on standard metaphoric inferences of kinship terms to illuminate the system; he calls on components of a well-known and deeply understood concept—genealogy—to illuminate his subject. Yet in some crucial ways, genealogy fails to match his subject, and this obliges him to modify explicitly the concept he calls up as a source domain for the metaphor. The poetic development derives in its structure from the tandem task of using the source domain to illuminate the system while modifying the source domain to prevent conflicts. Indeed, explicit modification of the source domain is a species of illumination, for the reader thus understands both wherein the two concepts naturally match and wherein modification is required to produce a match.

How do the metaphoric inferences operate in this passage from Milton? First, I will unpack Milton's subtle and interwoven uses of the *inheritance* inference. Sin and Death, as offspring of Satan, *inherit* key components; the poet relies on the expectation of similarity between parent and child to express the homomorphic parts of this infernal trinity. Sin, speaking to Satan, recalls that at her birth she was "Likest to thee in shape and count'nance bright," implying that proud Satan and arresting Sin share attractiveness, share the ostensible appearance—ephemeral and illusory—of power and vitality, of command and self-possession, of that naturalness and health and light that seem to characterize the expressions and gestures of the naturally privileged and self-reliant. There is a sensuality in confidence and command, an aristocratic attractiveness based on (1) the viewer's hope that through attachment he can participate in the confidence and

the latent power it suggests, and (2) the feeling that attention from such a source constitutes a high compliment, a partial ennobling. These qualities account for Satan's ability to
suborn a third of Heaven's angels into his company. The
power and ennoblement his presence seems to promise were
illusory, as the fallen angels no doubt knew at the time:
Milton's fallen Spirits habitually refer to the omnipotence of
God, often referring to him as the Almighty. Yet Satan's
appearance, his countenance bright, seduced them. Sin
inherits this component of Satan exactly: souls, often well-
apprised of the ultimate but for the moment abstract and
insignificant futility of seeking power or lasting pleasure or
confidence or ease from Sin, are nonetheless induced into
following her because her appearance falsely indicates qualities she in fact lacks. Herein lies the deceptive attraction of
both Satan and Sin.

Milton uses the father-daughter relation between Satan
and Sin to render and explore the nature of Satan and
thereby to teach the reader about the motives, nature, and
mechanics of separation from God. Concretely, the father-
daughter relation gives us two distinct ways to see how
Satan's attraction to Sin reveals the nature of his evil. The
first depends upon connotations of the father-daughter relation and the second upon *inheritance.*

Behavioral rights and constraints attach to the father-
daughter kinship relation, the chief constraint being the
incest taboo. Satan's violation of this taboo is an outright
violation of a natural order we ascribe to kinship. This violation of natural order dictated by divine order serves at once
as both a specific. instance and a general emblem of Satan's
violation of divine order.

The second path to understanding the attraction of Satan
to Sin as a manifestation of his rebellion against divine order
is supplied by *inheritance.* What is the nature of Satan's evil,
and just how does the kinship relation help us see it? The
preeminent sin of Satan is pride and excessive self-impor-
tance, born of excessive self-love. Both the pride and the
self-love are avatars of his more general sin of rebellion
against divine order, against his assigned place within it, and
against the love and obedience he owes to the creator of that
order. *Inheritance* implies that Sin shares components with

Satan, specifically his deluding attractiveness. She mirrors him, and therefore we can understand his attraction to her as a manifestation of his excessive self-love. He is attracted to himself in her. More profoundly, his attraction represents his absorption with himself and with images of himself rather than with divine order and its images. Sin states explicitly to Satan: "Thyself in me thy perfect image viewing / Becam'st enamor'd." This shows him captured by his own localized and ultimately self-defeating powers, which are nonetheless violent and momentarily overwhelming. Both the illusory attractiveness of Sin and his lust for her—two avatars of one feeling—symbolize Satanic powers: both enthrall momentarily; both involve self-concern and self-love; both become ultimately repugnant, as the text demonstrates. Satan, first meeting Sin at the Gate of Hell, finds her detestable: "I know thee not, nor ever saw till now / Sight more detestable than him and thee."

Milton's reliance on the *inheritance* inference also serves other, somewhat subtler purposes. It allows us to understand the career of the sinner, to understand the self-perception of the sinner and his process of degradation. Throughout the Satan-Sin-Death episode, we see not only that Satan's previous complicity with Sin persists, but more, that he feels compelled by his previous sinful act, by his having parented Sin, to confront her, acknowledge her, and ally himself even more strongly and abidingly to her. (His only alternative would be to accept his position in Hell by declining further involvement with Sin.) And this all transpires *even though* Sin's attractiveness, *inherited* from Satan, turns foul. When he first coupled with Sin, she appeared desirable to him; but now, after the fact and the consequences of that union, her repellent, deceiving, "double-form'd" nature is so evident to Satan that he fails at first to recognize her:

> What thing thou art, thus double-form'd, and why
> In this Infernal Vale first met thou call'st
> Me Father, and that Phantasm call'st my Son?
> I know thee not, nor ever saw till now
> Sight more detestable than him and thee.

But her power and appearance are an *inheritance* from him and hence a model of his own power and appearance.

Therefore, we can understand that his appearance and power must have also changed, that his appearance too must have degraded. There is evidence of the degradation of Satan's appearance and power throughout *Paradise Lost*, until even he sees it at book 9, line 487. Some of that evidence begins to appear in this episode. But there is more. As Sin, a model of Satan, does not notice the extent of the degradation which renders her unrecognizable until she names herself, so Satan does not notice the extent of his own degradation, which likewise prevents him from being recognized as what he thinks he appears to be. And so, just as Satan fails at first to treat Sin as Sin expects, Death correspondingly had failed at first to treat Satan as Satan expects. Indeed, Death sought to intimidate Satan:

> The Monster moving onward came as fast,
> With horrid strides.

Sin's plea to Satan, based on what she conceives to be her status as daughter and mother of his offspring, a status he at first does not recognize, mirrors Satan's earlier speech—a command and a threat to Death—which is similarly based on what Satan conceives to be his status. Notice Satan's presumptions about his status in his speech to Death:

> Whence and what are thou, execrable shape,
> That dar'st, though grim and terrible, advance
> Thy miscreated Front athwart my way
> To yonder Gates? through them *I mean to pass,*
> *That be assured, without leave askt of thee:*
> *Retire, or taste thy folly, and learn by proof,*
> *Hell-born, not to contend with Spirits of Heav'n.**

But here we see clearly in Death's retort that Satan's appearance and status have degraded. Responding as Satan will to Sin, Death claims not to recognize Satan's status:

> Art thou that Traitor Angel, art thou hee,
> Who first broke peace in Heav'n and Faith, till then

---

*When multiple-word phrases are italicized, it is because I wish to emphasize them. When single nouns are italicized, it is because they are italicized in *Paradise Lost*.

Unbrok'n, and in proud rebellious Arms
Drew after him the third part of Heav'n's Sons
Conjur'd against the Highest, for which both Thou
And they outcast from God, are here condemn'd
To waste Eternal days in woe and pain?
And reck'n'st thou thyself with Spirits of Heav'n,
Hell-doom'd, and breath'st defiance here and scorn,
Where I reign King, and to enrage thee more,
Thy King and Lord? Back to thy punishment,
False fugitive, and to thy speed add wings,
Lest with a whip of Scorpions I pursue
Thy ling'ring, or with one stroke of this Dart
Strange horror seize thee, and pangs unfelt before.

Like Sin, Satan is surprised at not being seen as the high thing he thinks he appears. As Sin, who perceived herself as attractive and the holder of certain powers, will be told that she is not recognized as either, so Satan, who sees himself as forbidding and pre-eminent in rule, is told that he is dismissable and in fact subject to the power he confronts. And more, as Satan speaks truly of Sin's status, so Death has spoken truly of Satan's, as Sin herself explains:

But thou O Father, I forewarn thee, shun
His deadly arrow; *neither vainly hope*
To be invulnerable in those bright Arms,
Though temper'd heav'nly, for that mortal dint,
Save he who reigns above, none can resist.

The appearance and power of Satan and of Sin undergo similar degradations; by seeing one as *inherited* from the parent by the child, and hence homomorphic, we can understand one as a model of the other and both as allegorizations of the same occurrence.

I have more to say later about the relationship between Satan and Sin, but here let us remain with *inheritance* as it applies to Death, also Satan's offspring. Death, like his father Satan and his mother Sin, is a power over mankind, and over all but holy spirits. From Satan, Death *inherits* his disdain. Satan views Death with disdain and himself as Lord:

Th' undaunted Fiend what this might be admir'd,
Admir'd, not fear'd; God and his son except,
Created thing naught valu'd he nor shunn'd;
And *with disdainful look* thus first began.

Death *inherits* the disdain and the sense of power:

and breath'st defiance here and scorn,
Where I reign King, and to enrage thee more,
Thy King and Lord? Back to thy punishment,
False fugitive, and to thy speed add wings.

Like Satan, Death stands ready to enforce his intention, regardless of the adversary. Milton evokes the image of father and son standing in partial mirror reflection, and our understanding of that mirroring relies upon our concept of the *inheritance* of properties. I will have to quote the entire passage to show the elaborate balancing of father against son. Milton begins with Death, and then balances Satan against him:

So spake [Death] the grisly terror, and in shape,
So speaking and so threat'ning, grew tenfold
More dreadful and deform: *on th'other side*
Incens't with indignation *Satan* stood
Unterrifi'd, and like a Comet burn'd,
That fires the length of *Ophiucus* huge
In th' Artic Sky, and from his horrid hair
Shakes Pestilence and War.

At this point, Milton has established the mirroring through *inheritance* so firmly that no distinction need be made between Satan and Death; each subsequent description refers to both simultaneously:

Each at the Head
Levell'd his deadly aim; thir fatal hands
No second stroke intend, and such a frown
Each cast at th'other, as when two black Clouds
With Heav'n's Artillery fraught, come rattling on
Over the *Caspian*, then stand front to front
Hov'ring a space, till Winds the signal blow
To join thir dark Encounter in mid air:
So frown'd the mighty Combatants, that Hell

Grew darker at their frown, so matcht they stood:
For never but once more was either like
To meet so great a foe.

As Satan burns like a comet when provoked, so Death grows ten times more dreadful and deformed: each exaggerates the particular emblem of his latent power. Throughout the balance of the passage, they perform identical actions.

Indeed, Death, as his father Satan has done, challenges his own father, and in doing so he partially repeats a pattern Satan, as type, has laid down. In both cases, the son ultimately assumes an existence, a defined status, according to the judgment of his father. God damns Satan, and this judgment confines Satan to only those roles his father will allow, however rebellious or powerful the son may be. Similarly, Satan, knowing the nature of Death, speaks exactly those words needed to confine Death to the role Satan wishes him to play, however powerful the son. To show all this will be tricky, because Milton's text is tricky. The crucial occurrences are Satan's attempt to manipulate Death by speaking to Sin in Death's hearing, and Sins's response, likewise witnessed by Death. As I give these two passages, I will discuss the interworkings of *inheritance, functional property transfer*, and idealized cognitive models of kin. I will then take up other parts of the Satan-Sin-Death episode to pursue the details of these idealized cognitive models and show how they work throughout the scene. In particular, I will clarify that it is not the theological allegory but rather idealized cognitive models of kin that provide the model for certain key moments in the episode. I will then return to deepen the discussion of the *inheritance* inference in relation to Satan and his offspring, before moving to a discussion of the relation between Sin and Death.

Let us begin with Satan trying to persuade Death and Sin by speaking to Sin in Death's hearing:

Dear Daughter, since thou claim'st me for thy Sire,
And my fair Son here shows't me . . .
　　　　. . . know
I come no enemy, but to set free
From out this dark and dismal house of pain,
Both him and thee, and all the heav'nly Host

Of Spirits that in our just pretenses arm'd
Fell with us from on high: from them *I go*
This uncouth errand sole, and one for all
Myself expose . . .
    . . . I . . .
    . . . shall soon return,
And bring ye to the place where Thou and Death
Shall dwell at ease, and up and down unseen
Wing silently the buxom Air, imbalm'd
With odors; there ye shall be fed and fill'd
Immeasurably, all things shall be your prey.
He ceas'd, for both seem'd highly pleas'd, and Death
Grinn'd horrible a ghastly smile, to hear
His famine should be fill'd, and blest his maw
Destin'd to that good hour: no less rejoic'd
His mother bad.

By the end of this passage, Sin and Death are persuaded.
Our acceptance and comprehension of the process of their
persuasion relies on our understanding that Sin and Death
have *inherited* from Satan a blinding self-interest which permits them to act on hopes whose ultimate vanity they know
full well. Just as Satan rebels against God's plans and against
his own divinely determined station when he knows God
cannot be thwarted, when he knows that nothing can tran-
spire without the permission of God, so Sin and Death—
despite Sin's previous references to the omnipotence of Fate
and the Almighty—rebel against their assigned stations as
keepers of the gate, hoping to gain more for themselves than
God has intended for them, believing, in their *inherited*
blind self-interest, that they can outwit the will of God, as
Sin shows in her response:

The key of this infernal Pit by due,
And by command of Heav'n's all-powerful King
I keep, by him forbidden to unlock
These Adamantine Gates; against all force
Death ready stands to interpose his dart,
Fearless to be o'ermatcht by living might.
But what owe I to his commands above
Who hates me, and hath hither thrust me down
Into this gloom of *Tartarus* profound,

To sit in hateful Office here confin'd,
Inhabitant of Heav'n, and heav'nly-born,
Here in perpetual agony and pain,
With terrors and with clamors compasst round
Of mine own brood, that on my bowels feed:
Thou art my Father, thou my Author, thou
My being gav'st me; whom should I obey
But thee, whom follow? thou wilt bring me soon
To that new world of light and bliss, among
The Gods who live at ease, *where I shall Reign*
At thy right hand voluptuous, *as beseems*
Thy daughter and thy darling, without end.
Thus saying, from her side the fatal Key,
Sad instrument of all our woe, she took.

Satan has moved them because they have *inherited* his ability for self-deception. For example, he claimed they "Shall dwell at ease," and Sin echoes, "thou wilt bring me soon / To that new world of light and bliss, among / The Gods who live at ease." They have *inherited* his self-interests, such as the desire to rule, and he has used those common interests to move them. He says, "all things shall be your prey," and Sin echoes, "I shall reign / At thy right hand," and Death "Grinn'd horrible a ghastly smile, to hear / His famine should be fill'd, and blest his maw." Satan perceives himself as heavenly but thrust down, first when Jesus appears in Heaven and again when Satan is cast into Hell. He perceives himself as belonging to a supremely high natural rank which the divine order denies, and consequently he rebels against his confinement, whether in Heaven or Hell or Earth or Chaos. Sin *inherits*, and thereby mirrors and models, this self-perception as heavenly but thrust down, as belonging to a high natural rank denied by divine order. She claims God "hath hither thrust me down / . . . / To sit in hateful Office here confin'd, / Inhabitant of Heav'n, and heav'nly born." She speaks of the lofty rank she feels she merits ("I shall Reign . . . as beseems"). She also *inherits*, as the consequence of this perception, rebellion against divine order: she rejects God and her divinely appointed station and opens for Satan and Death the gates between Hell and Earth. This is beautifully apt. Sin should *inherit* rebellion against divine order; sin is by definition rebellion against divine order.

The second main inference operating in this encounter is *functional property transfer*. In their confrontation, Satan and Death behave toward each other in a pattern of kinship behavior familiar to us all as father-son conflict and which in this case might arguably be called Oedipal: indeed, the father does not recognize his son or pay him due respect, which vexes the son. We have idealized cognitive models of (1) the father thwarting the son, (2) the son destroying the father in a moment of violence (as in *Oedipus Tyrranos* or the myth of Zeus and Kronos), and (3) the father swaying the son, who, immature, in fact outpowers his father but postpones the use of that power. The first behavior obtains between God and Satan and is the stereotypical behavior where father and young son have trenchantly opposed self-interests. The second is a potential and threatened behavior between Satan and Death, and Milton relies on our knowledge of this model to produce the tension in the confrontation. But Sin intercedes to transform this potential second behavior into the third behavior, which is typical between son and father who have some compelling common interests.

In the intercession by Sin we see a point where a stereotypical behavior attaching to the kinship relations of wife and daughter overtakes for a moment the theological allegory. Sin intercedes between conflicting father and son, Satan and Death, and she does so in the name of daughter and mother. It might plausibly be argued that, in the abstract allegory, Sin knows that they all three are doomed and that it is her place then to remind Satan and Death of the common bonds of their infernal nature and of their common damnation, whereas Satan and Death, active powers, may be bloated by a false sense of power and may need to be reminded of this common bond. Perhaps this is true; the theological allegory fits. But it is very weak as allegory, and there are counterarguments to this justification. First, Sin in fact forgets her doom and hopes to rebel against her divinely appointed station. Second, she is in fact a great power herself in the allegory, only slightly less inevitable as a power over man than Death: she overcame Satan in Heaven and has power to keep Death at bay:

And me his Parent would full soon devour
For want of other prey, but that he knows
His end with mine involv'd; and knows that I
Should prove a bitter Morsel, and his bane,
Whenever that shall be.

I think that kinship rather than allegory principally gives the model for the intercession. We have a stereotype of women-folk interceding when males in a family—particularly father and son—conflict. Women remind the adversaries of kinship ties, of behavior expected of kin standing in a certain relation, of enduring common interests. Sin follows this pattern exactly. With hideous outcry she rushes between; she calls Satan "Father" and Death "Son," and repeats the appellations as a kind of invocation of duty between kin, as if to define their roles for them. She chastises Satan for intending harm to his son and Death for the youthful fury that causes him to rise against his father. She then in explicit detail delineates their common position and interest. And it is her voice, the feminine voice of daughter, wife, and mother, that arrests them:

O Father, what intends thy hand, she cri'd,
Against thy only Son? What fury O Son,
Possesses thee to bend that mortal Dart
Against thy Father's head? and know'st for whom;
For him who sits above and laughs the while
At thee ordain'd his drudge, to execute
Whate'er his wrath, which he calls Justice, bids,
His wrath which one day will destroy ye both.
She spake, and at her words the hellish Pest
Forbore, then these to her *Satan* return'd:
So strange thy outcry, and thy words so strange
Thou interposest, that my sudden hand
Prevented spares to tell thee yet by deeds
What it intends.

Note further that in their acquiescence to Satan, the *behaviors* of Death and Sin differ in ways we can understand as the different expected *behaviors* of son and daughter-wife. Death must be persuaded that acquiescence serves his self-interest; yet Sin, though explicitly arguing their common self-interest, nonetheless adjoins stereotypical expressions of daughterly and wifely submission and naive trust:

> Thou art my Father, thou my Author, thou
> My being gav'st me; whom should I obey
> But thee, whom follow? thou wilt bring me soon
> To that new world of light and bliss, among
> The Gods who live at ease, where I shall Reign
> At thy right hand voluptuous, as beseems
> Thy daughter and thy darling, without end.

Inheritance is a general term with particular meanings for each particular parent-child relationship. Sin is the daughter of Satan while Death is the son, resulting in different bequests. Both *inherit* power. Death is active, and imposes itself (usually) against the will and desire of man. Its methods need not be appealing. Sin's power, however, is much more passive and stereotypically feminine: she seduces, beguiles, enthralls, entices. Souls must join with her for her to have effect. Seen this way, Death and Sin *inherit* different aspects of the power of Satan. God and his son excepted, Satan held the strongest and most compelling power, in battle using coercion and destruction: this aspect Death *inherits*. Yet of all spirits, Satan was the most beautiful, the most to be admired; his magnificence of bearing and speech seduce. This seductive appearance, unreflective of inner iniquity, gives him a twofold nature of outward desirability and consequent, hidden foulness: this aspect Sin *inherits*.

Now let us begin to look at the very odd relationship between Sin and Death. Principally, it depends upon the metaphoric inference *causation*. Theologically, the existence of original sin accounts for our physical death, and individual sin can produce individual spiritual death. The ascendency of Death over Satan and the creation of Death are the consequences of Satan's disobedience, indeed of his involvement with Sin. Disobedience has within it the seed of death for it violates divine order, and this violation alone brings about death.

At certain points in this extended use of kinship metaphor, particularly in this relationship between Sin and Death, the metaphor fits the system to be presented only weakly or with conflict, and the poet concerns himself, while he relies on similarities, also to demarcate the differences. Some points of poor fit are obvious, others more subtle. Obvious examples are the behaviors of Death and Sin toward each other and the behavior of the yelling monsters toward their mother. Sin loathes her son ("this odious offspring"). His birth deforms her ("breaking violent way / Tore through my entrails, that with fear and pain / Distorted, all my nether shape thus grew / Transform'd"). She regards him as an enemy, and he threatens to kill her ("but he my inbred enemy / Forth issu'd, brandishing his fatal Dart / Made to destroy"). Milton pointedly portrays Death as swifter and stronger than Sin, as overcoming Sin against her will, as raping her:

> I fled, but he pursu'd (though more, it seems,
> Inflam'd with lust than rage) and swifter far,
> Mee overtook his mother all dismay'd,
> And in embraces forcible and foul
> Ingend'ring with me.

Death is in fact a foe who desires to devour his mother but fears her:

> Before mine eyes in opposition sits
> Grim *Death* my Son and foe, who sets them on,
> And me his Parent would full soon devour.

These aspects of the relation between Sin and Death, none suggested by kinship as metaphor, some compatible with it, some requiring us to modify kinship and view the behavior as strange for kin in this relation, derive not from kinship as metaphor but rather from the conceptual allegory: Sin does not desire Death to be its consequence; the attractiveness of Sin is deformed by its result, Death; Sin would like to live as Sin, free from Death, able to escape Death, but Death comes swiftly and strongly upon her. The rape of Sin by Death produces monstrosities incompatible with idealized cognitive models of kin:

> These yelling Monsters that with ceaseless cry
> Surround me, as thou saw'st, *hourly conceiv'd*
> *And hourly born, with sorrow infinite*

To me, for when they list, into the womb
That bred them they return, and howl and gnaw
My Bowels, thir repast; then bursting forth
Afresh with conscious terrors vex me round,
That rest or intermission none I find.

Again, kinship does not suggest this behavior, and we must modify our stereotypes of kinship behavior in order to accommodate it. The behavior of the monsters results not from kinship metaphor but from the theological allegory, though there is room for confusion in interpreting the allegory. The monsters might be taken allegorically as the particular instances of the general concept of sin or as the specific behavior or mental sins produced by a general psychological state of sinfulness as opposed to piety, but more likely the monsters are the anguishing consequences of Sin contemplating Death. Their behavior and torture of Sin, and their encouragement by Death, suggest the torments of the sinner, particularly gnawing guilt and fear. (Actually, our stereotype of incest as unnatural makes it easy to see incestuous offspring as unnatural and exceptional; if we think of this as we read this passage, then we have an excuse, perhaps even a motivation, for the modification. In that case, the theological allegory fits with the underlying incestuous-kinship metaphor better.)

The genealogies of Sin and Death are themselves unusual and not entailed by idealized cognitive models of kinship. Satan engenders his own sin and his own death. More generally, pride and turning from divine order engender both the sin of disobedience and the possibility of death. Thus, to fit the allegory, Satan must parent both Sin and Death. Yet, though denial of divine order results in both Sin and Death, death is regarded as a consequence of sin: the first is the punishment which arises and waits when the second is committed. So Sin must parent Death. The only way stereotypical kinship relations can be modified to fit the conceptual allegory is to make Sin both the offspring and mate of Satan, as Milton does. This alteration serves some of his other purposes, and we are treated to a compendious and harmonious dovetailing of several meanings and effects within one structure.

An even sharper display of the match and mismatch of allegory and kinship occurs in Milton's narrative of the birth of Sin, which Sin relates to Satan when he fails to recognize her. She sprang from his head:

All on a sudden miserable pain
Surpris'd thee, dim thine eyes, and dizzy swum
In darkness, while thy head flames thick and fast
Threw forth, till on the left side op'ning wide,
Likest to thee in shape and count'nance bright,
Then shining heav'nly fair, a Goddess arm'd
Out of thy head I sprung

In the theology behind this, Satan conceives of rebelling against divine order ("In bold conspiracy against Heav'n's King"), which means he conceives of sin. This is allegorized as Satan's mental events giving birth to a daughter, Sin. That he is revolted at her birth ("amazement seiz'd / All th' Host of Heav'n; back they recoil'd afraid / At first") violates connotations of kinship metaphor and must be forcibly imported from the theological allegory. Milton gets help in this through another trick I will discuss in a moment. But aside from the revulsion at the offspring, Satan's mental occurrences almost beg to be expressed through kinship metaphor. As I hinted in chapter 2, and as I will analyze fully in chapter 4, the *causation as progeneration* inference of kinship metaphor is a fundamental tool for understanding mental events and in particular the conception of ideas or intentions. Satan conceives of Sin, and therefore Sin exists. (This is implicit in the Biblical term for Satan as "liar and [therefore] father of lies" [John 8:44], borrowed later by Dante [*bugiardo, e padre di menzogna* at *Inferno* 23:144]. It also recalls the doctrine in Zoroastrianism that since Ahura-Mazda creates by means of thought and since he foresees the evil Angra Mainyu, Evil comes into existence.) Parentage is an apt vehicle to express mental conception. But, as in most cases of mental progeneration, the offspring (Sin) has only one parent (Satan), and this exemplifies the main mismatch between genealogy and (mental) causation as progeneration. In a flashing brief application of kinship metaphor, the second parent can be ignored. But in extended uses, as here, something must be done to explain the absence of the other parent. Milton's expedient, drawn from Hesiod and also used by Blake, is to invent an unusual process of birth from a single parent. In this case, as in Hesiod (where Athena is born from the brow of Zeus), a headache signals the mental conception, and the birth is a leaping of the offspring fully grown from the head. Milton in fact takes pains to highlight the shock and monstrosity of such an aberrant birth ("dim thine eyes, and dizzy swum / In darkness, while thy head flames thick and fast / Threw forth"), because he needs that shock and monstrosity to block other connotations of kinship, such as that adults love infants, that no adult fears an infant, and that newborn infants are absolutely innocent, defenseless, and without guile.

It may by now seem obvious that the coherence of this episode from Milton relies on a mapping between the target domain of theology and the source domain of kinship. The source domain has its own elaborate structure, connotations, and metaphoric inferences which the author must acknowledge and use for the purposes of his message. This appears to have been overlooked by the Milton critics I have read. They give a variety of different responses to the question, What is it that motivates the selection of kinship as the domain of the metaphor, and what are the consequences of that selection?

Some critics, like William Empson, Burton Weber, Roland Frye, and, to some extent, Anne Ferry, give the theological meaning of the allegory without exploring how we can understand the metaphor as delivering that meaning. How does this source domain, kinship, fit that theological system? The events of the passage are not factitious. Milton could not simply invent events to be interpreted as allegory without his being strongly constrained and empowered by the place of those events in the domain of kinship.

Other critics motivate the events in this passage by giving analogues. J. B. Broadbent claims "Allegory must rely on a convention, but here is a baffling confusion of analogues" (p. 126). He then explains that Milton's Sin is Spenser's Error, that she is related to Cerberus, Scylla, and medieval witches, that Death is described like Phineas Fletcher's Sin, and so on. He explains the birth of sin by finding sources in the Psalms, and the relation of Satan, Sin, and Death by pointing to a source in James. This scholarship is admirable, but it is a mistake to judge the cohesion of a metaphor by locating possible analogues. That merely pushes the question back a step: What is the metaphoric structure of the analogues? That an author has many sources, or none, for his metaphor tells us very little or nothing about the structure and quality of the extended conceptual metaphor he offers. It is similarly interesting that, as Francis Blessington and John Steadman show, Satan's behavior has analogues in classical heroes, notably Odysseus; or, as Arthur Dobbins shows, that much about Sin and Death seems to be drawn from Revelation; or, as several critics mention, that many components of this passage parody other texts (Satan as parody of Odysseus, Satan-Sin-Death as parody of the Trinity, Sin's vows of obedience as parody of Jesus's), which can help us interpret the allegory when these texts parodied concern theology. But none of this illuminates the structure of the metaphor. None of it tells us how kinship works in the metaphor. This lacuna is characteristic of literary criticism.

Human condition: Satan, Sin, Death, and Vice in Gower

In a text quite different from Milton's in the circumstances and allegorical meanings of the genealogy it unfolds, John Gower earlier used kinship metaphor to capture the relations of Satan, Sin, Death, and Vice. But of course this text too relies for its understanding on the reader's knowledge of a handful of metaphoric inferences of kinship terms, and of stereotypical connotations attached to those kinship terms. This permits us to see by parallax, through two clearly different kinship-metaphoric castings of the same subject matter, the common metaphoric inferences underlying them. An alleged source for Milton's episode, Gower's rendering in lines 204-76 of *Mirour de l'omme* (ed. G. A. Macaulay, 1899) presents Satan as outright unmotivated evil. There seems to lie behind him no process of fall from grace and hence no complicated psychology. The creation of Sin and the union of Sin and Death derive from Satan's conscious and malicious planning. Death does not overcome Sin, nor, in general, do the family members feel tensions between themselves or their respective self-interests. No pain or damage attends the births. And, in general, surprise, revelation, and recognition have no place in the tale. Consequently, Gower's allegory lacks the depth of meaning of Milton's. But the same few metaphoric inferences of kinship terms allow us to interpret his allegory. I will begin with the passage in which Gower lays out the genealogy and show how it depends upon *lineage, functional property transfer,* and *inheritance.* I give a prose crib, followed by the original in parentheses:

[Heading:] How Sin was born of the devil, and how Death was born of Sin, and how Death married his mother, and engendered upon her the seven deadly sins. [Verse:] The devil, who contrives all evils, and hates and reviles every good, out of his malice conceived and then produced a daughter, who was very evil, ugly, and vile, who was named Sin. He also was her nurse, and guarded her, and taught her of his most treacherous guile, wherefor the daughter for her part became so violent that nothing she touched was not defiled. His young daughter, for her part, so kept the devil in pleasure and made him such pleasant entertainment that he was enamoured of her so much that upon his daughter he engendered a son, who was named Death. Then the devil had great comfort because he thought that by their influence he would have his will over men; for when the two are in accord, whatever comes into their power the devil gains.

([Heading:] Comment Pecché nasquist du deble, et comment Mort nasquist du Pecché, et comment Mort espousa sa miere et engendra sur luy les sept vices mortieux. [Verse:] Ly deable, qui tous mals soubtile / Et trestous biens hiet et revile, / De sa malice concevoit / Et puis enfantoit une file, / Q'ert tresmalvoise, laide et vile, / La quelle Pecché noun avoit. / Il mesmes sa norrice estoit, / Et la gardoit et doctrinoit / De sa plus tricherouse guile; / Par quoy la file en son endroit / Si violente devenoit, / Que riens ne touch que n'avile. / Tant perservoit le deble a gré / Sa jofne file en son degré / Et tant luy fist plesant desport, / Dont il fuist tant enamouré, / Que sur sa file ad engendré / Un fils, que l'en appella Mort. / Lors ot le deable grant confort, / Car tout quidoit par leur enhort / De l'ome avoir sa volenté; / Car quant ils deux sont d'un accort, / Tout quanque vient a leur resort / Le deble tient enherité.) (ll. 204-28)

In this passage, Satan conceives Sin out of his malice: this is *lineage*. That is, the Feeling (malice) affects Behavior (sin), and this Behavior, sin, is expressed metaphorically as the offspring of the Feeling. The *lineage* inference permits Gower, like Milton, to dispense with a female parent for sin: the generation of sin is world-mind-behavior progeneration, and the familiarity of single parentage in world-mind-behavior progeneration makes the second parent optional.

Functional property transfer underlies Satan's behavior toward Sin. In bearing Sin ("enfantoit"), Satan *behaves* as an androgynous parent. In teaching and rearing her, he *behaves* as both parent and nurse. Sin also *inherits* her attributes from her parent ("tresmalvoise, laide et vile"). Though Gower and Milton have Satan bequeath different qualities to Sin, both Gower and Milton rely on our understanding of *inheritance* in general to account for Sin's resultant attributes.

Missing from Gower's allegory are the explicit interpretation of Satan's attraction to Sin as a brand of self-love and the depicting of Sin as superficially beautiful and beguiling but ultimately repulsive. In Gower, Satan simply finds his ugly daughter Sin agreeable and desirable because Gower's Satan likes ugliness and sin. Milton's Satan undergoes human desires, blindness, and ultimate repulsion; Gower's Satan thinks and feels in ways much thinner and much further removed from humanity.

Gower then employs various metaphoric inferences to convey the Satan-Sin-Death group and their interworkings as one body, whose members have similar interests, and who form a kind of clan. First, the clan must be enlarged:

Sin the daughter and Death the son were very dear to their father, for they resembled him greatly: and for this, by his design, in order to have more offspring, the mother married (espousa) her child: thus seven children were engendered, who are the heirs of hell and have dismayed the world; as I will describe to you, telling by what names people call them and of the offices in which they are instructed. The names of the children of Sin, one after another in their rank I will tell, of whom the first was named Pride, he was the eldest, the very evil and unhappy, who most resembled his false father.

(Au piere furont molt cheris / Pecché sa file et Mort son fils, / Car trop luy furont resemblant: / Et pour cela par son devis, / Pour plus avoir de ses norris, / La miere espousa son enfant: / Si vont sept files engendrant, / Qui sont d'enfern enheritant / Et ont le mond tout entrepris; / Come je vous serray devisant, / Des queux nouns om leur est nomant / Et du mestier dont sont apris. / Les nouns des files du Pecché / L'un apres l'autre en leur degré / Dirray, des quelles la primere / Orguil ad noun, celle est l'aisnée, / La tresmalvoise maluré, / Que plus resemble a son fals piere.) (ll. 229-46)

As I mentioned, this conception of Satan, Sin, and Death differs from the one we saw in Milton: no headache, no deformed and double-formed daughter-mother, no seduction turned repulsion, no titanic confrontation between father and son, no division of interests, no deceptive oratory, no complicated blindness and self-delusion, no mother-raping, no yapping monsters crawling back up into the womb of an anguished mother to gnaw her entrails. But the metaphoric inferences are all here: Sin and Death please Satan because they resemble him so so ("Car trop luy furont resemblant"); this is *inheritance*. Satan's interest in power has been *inherited* by his progeny. The seven offspring of Sin and Death *inherit* the infernal nature of the family line ("Qui sont d'enfern enheritant"). We saw already in Milton how different Satanic qualities are *inherited* by Sin and Death. *Inheritance* can partition attributes—a concept quite familiar to us and evidenced in the genre of recognition statements like: "He's got his father's temper," "She's got her grandmother's eyes," and so on. Gower relies on this notion of *inheritance* as a partitioning of attributes in order to present the seven deadly sins as a partitioning of sin and of general Satanism. There is a stereotype of the firstborn as preeminent heir of familial traits, a stereotype much more common in an age of primogeniture and fitting Gower's desire to invoke the concept of a feudal family. Gower explicitly calls up this stereotype ("Que plus resemble a son fals piere"). The first child of Sin *inherits* the preeminent sin of her father—pride. The other deadly sins, *inheriting* other aspects of Satanism (Envy, Ire, Avarice, Sloth, Gluttony, and Lechery), are presented in a catalog I will skip.

Gower then pursues an extended elaboration of the feudal

aristocratic family as a metaphor for the behaviors of Satan,
Sin, Death, and the seven deadly sins:

> . . . the other seven, who are subject to attend the devil;
> wherefore he who advances all evils, when he saw such
> offspring born, rejoiced for his part greatly. [Heading:] How
> the devil sent Sin with her seven children to the world, and
> how he held his parliament about how to entrap man.
> [Verse:] The devil, who is full of rage, when he saw that he
> had such a great lineage, sent them to the world: Sin the
> foolish and wild conveyed her children of whoredom to the
> world. And such was made and contrived there that the
> false world inclined to do all according to their training;
> through them she devised her glory, through them she
> advised always, through them she made much horrible
> outrage. Each one according to his place had a secular
> office, to entrap the world more: Pride maintained her glory,
> Envy continually advised her, and Ire was her warrior, and
> Avarice her treasurer, and Sloth was her chamberlain, and
> Gluttony of his right was master butler, and Lechery in his
> office was above all her dear friend. He who engenders all
> evils, when he saw the children of his line bring the world to
> their will, began to take counsel how man could be seized,
> he who before had caused the beautiful estate of paradise to
> fall.

(Ly autre sept, que d'attendance / Au deble sont par tout
soubgit; / Dont cil qui tous les mals avance, / Quant naistre
vit ytiele enfance, / De sa part grantment s'esjoit. / [Head-
ing:] Comment le deable envoya Pecché, ovesque ses sept
files au Siecle, et comment il tient puis son parlement, pour
l'omme enginer. [Verse:] Ly deable, q'est tout plain du rage,
/ Quant vist qu'il ot si grant lignange, / Au Siecle tous les
envoia: / Pecché la fole et la salvage / Ses propres files du
putage / Parmy le Siecle convoia; / Et tant y fist et engina /
Que ly fals Siecle s'enclina / De fair tout par leur menage, /
Par ceaux sa gloire devisa, / Par ceaux toutdis se conseila, /
Par ceaux fist maint horrible oultrage. / Chascune solone son
endroit / Office seculiere avoit / Le Siecle pour plus enginer:
/ Orguil sa gloire maintenoit, / Envie ades luy consailloit, /
Et d'Ire fist son guerroier, / Et d'Avarice tresorer, / Accidie

estoit son chamberer, / Et Glotonie de son droit / Estoit son
maistre boteller, / Et Leccherie en son mestier / Sur tous sa
chiere amie estoit. / Cil qui trestous ceos mals engendre, /
Quant vist les files de son gendre / Mener le Siecle a leur
voloir, / Lors comenca consail a prendre / Coment cel
homme pot susprendre, / Le quel devant ot fait chaoir /
Du paradis le beau Manoir.) (ll. 272-307)

Satan, seeing his offspring as a house, a clan, a lineage,
dispatches them to the terrestrial world, hoping to bring that
domain under his sway, to be ruled by his family business as
it were, and each of his offspring is delegated a particular
office, where the division of labor fits the idiosyncratic
talents of each. Relying on the *behaves-as* inference to convey the allegory, Gower invokes the stereotype of the clan,
the aristocratic house, the patriarchal and feudal family as a
political power, and asks the reader to see this Satanic group
as *behaving* in a manner stereotypically attached to our concept of such a feudal family. The power interests of Satan
have been *inherited* by his children, and he intends to rely on
them, as part of a political unit, to bring him gain: whatever
property falls to his children Sin and Death is ultimately part
of his estate: "for when the two are in accord, whatever
comes into their power the devil gains" ("Car quant ils deux
sont d'un accord, / Tout quanque vient a leur resort / Le
deble tient enherite"). This metaphor of Satan, Death, Sin,
and specified sins as a family of the nobility is extended
when they all meet in council to discuss strategy:

Sin the lady of the land with her seven noble children came
first to the assembly.

(Pecché la dame du paiis / Ove ses sept files noblement /
Vint primer a l'assemblement.) (ll. 341-44)

In the assembly, both Sin and Death *behave* as devoted
offspring, swearing allegiance to their father, and making his
cause their own. Satan speaks first, requesting allegiance,
and Sin answers:

"For this reason I ask you, if you are my friends, advise me
in this business, so that I might do thus." Sin his daughter
responded, thus she said her opinion first: "Father, you have

my certain faith, I will defraud the human flesh, with my seven children whom I raised."

("Par ceste cause je vous pri, / Sicomme vous m'estez tout amy, / Consailletz moy en cest ovraigne, / Au fin que porray faire ensi." / Pecché sa file respondi / Si dist sa resoun primeraine: / "Piere, tenez ma foy certain, / Je fray tricher la char humaine / Ove mes sept files q'ay norri") (ll. 361-69)

The terrestrial world also answers Satan. Then Death, very like a son in the aristocracy, promises to avenge his father:

"I will avenge you upon man."

("De l'omme je te vengeray") (l. 387)

Human condition: The curse on humanity in the Bible, Gower, and Milton

Milton's and Gower's Satan-Sin-Death texts exemplify the ubiquitous use of kinship as metaphor to create, structure, examine, and unpack components of Christianity. The Trinity itself is unthinkable in the absence of stereotypes of kin relations. To understand the Christian doctrine of guilt through original sin, we must refer to *inheritance*: man *inherits* the guilt of Adam. In fact, whether one perceives the Old Testament through Christianity, Judaism, historiography, folklore, or common love of narrative, *inheritance* will pervasively underlie one's understanding of the text. For example, Gower sees the curse on humanity and the serpent in Genesis 3 through Christian eyes and so gives the interpretation of it implicit in his re-telling of the tale. Milton concurs. The annotators of the *Oxford Annotated Bible* (1962) see the text through different eyes and so offer a different interpretation. But *inheritance* underlies all three interpretations, as I will show. Let's begin with Genesis 3:

God said to the serpent, "Because you have done this, cursed are you above all cattle, and above all wild animals; upon your belly you shall go, and dust you shall eat all the days of your life. I will put enmity between you and the woman, and between your seed and her seed; he shall bruise your head, and you shall bruise his heel." To the woman he said, "I will greatly multiply your pain in childbearing; in pain you shall bring forth children, yet your desire shall be for your husband, and he shall rule over you." And to Adam he said, "Because you have listened to the voice of your wife, and have eaten of the tree of which I commanded you, 'You shall not eat of it,' cursed is the ground because of you; in toil you shall eat of it all the days of your life; thorns and thistles it shall bring forth to you; and you shall eat the plants of the field. In the sweat of your face you shall eat bread till you return to the ground, for out of it you were taken; you are dust, and to dust you shall return." (Revised Standard Version)

Note that, except for the enmity between human beings and snakes, the Biblical passage nowhere states that offspring shall inherit this punishment. Yet there is no need to state it. It can be assumed. The concept of *inheritance* enables us to understand that the condition of a kind—be it serpent or man—is to be accounted for as the *inherited* condition of ancestral kin: serpents shall move on the ground; men and serpents will bear mutual natural enmity; childbirth shall be painful; woman shall have desire for her husband and be subordinate to him; the ground shall be cursed and work will become toil for men.

The annotators of the *Oxford Annotated Bible* grant all this tacitly, as if it is obvious in the text. Our use of kinship metaphor is so natural and frequent that we forget we are in fact applying it as a strong aid to understanding. But the annotators draw the line, in their interpretation, at the *inheritance* of death. "The punishment does not include death, for it is assumed that man is mortal; rather, because of man's estrangement from God death becomes an anxiety which haunts him until he dies" (p. 5).

This interpretation is rejected by Gower, a Christian, who explicitly cites death as the ultimate component of the punishment:

It was the judgment of God that Adam be basely thrust out of paradise into earth where in pain most sad his food and clothing he would go to procure and seek; his wife also for her transgression, wherein she did not wish to please God, always in her labor, when she came to natural business, must bring forth sons and daughters in weeping and groaning. But all this would have been no more than a game, if they had not had more pain; for the worst thing above all was death, wherefor they were lost in hell, far from God—the father and mother and daughter and son, without end to remain there always.

(C'estoit du dieu le Jugement, / Q'Adam serroit vilaynnement / Botuz du Paradis en terr; / U q'en dolour molt tristement / Sa viande et son vestement / Irroit a pourchacer et querre: / Sa femme auci pour son contrere, / De ce q'a dieu ne voloit plere, / Tous jours a son enfantement, / Quant vient au naturel affere, / Doit tous ses fils et files trere / En plour et en ghemissement. / Mais tout ce n'eust esté que jeeu, / Si plus du paine n'eust ëeu; / Mais sur trestout c'estoit le pis / La mort, dont au darrein perdu / Furont loigns en enfern de dieu / Et piere et miere et file et fils, / Sanz fin pour demourer toutdis.) (ll. 169-87)

Milton concurs that death is part of the punishment, and implies that death derives from the sin of Adam and Eve. The archangel Michael gives Adam a vision of the future, and of death and woe, so that Adam may "know / What misery th'inabstinence of Eve / Shall bring on men" (12.474-76). We understand this by figuring that the sin (inabstinence) results in the curse which sets conditions on Adam and Eve, and that those conditions are *inherited* by their progeny.

So though the source and its derivatives and its interpretations may all differ, yet they are unified by an underlying technique of understanding, *inheritance*, which is provided by kinship metaphor. In the minds of the generators of the texts, the interpreters of the texts, and the readers of the texts, *inheritance* served and serves as a powerful metaphor for casting meaning upon a domain.

Human condition: Psychology in Blake

The texts considered so far in this chapter concern components of the human condition. The components have been few and centered on the concept of sin. Blake presents a far more elaborate—indeed, often wild and obscure— genealogy of components of human psychology in a rough, unfinished, and incomplete manuscript work traditionally referred to by its first five words, "then She bore Pale desire." Though complicated, the work is so rewarding and rich in its use of kinship metaphor, so beautiful at the close if one appreciates the distilled essence of Blake's prophetic vision, and so hard to find in print, that I will quote it entirely from Erdman (1965):

then She bore Pale desire father of Curiosity a Virgin ever young. And after. Leaden Sloth from whom came Ignorance. who brought forth wonder. These are the Gods which Came from fear. for Gods like these. nor male nor female are but Single Pregnate or if they list together min- gling bring forth mighty powers[.] She knew them not yet they all war with Shame and Strengthen her weak arm. But Pride awoke nor knew that Joy was born. and taking Poisnous Seed from her own Bowels. in the Monster Shame infusd. forth Came Ambition Crawling like a toad Pride Bears it in her Bosom. and the Gods. all bow to it. So Great its Power. that Pride inspird by it Prophetic Saw the Kingdoms of the World & all their Glory. Giants of Mighty arm before the flood. Cains City. built with Murder. Then Babel mighty Reard him to the Skies. Babel with thousand tongues Confusion it was calld. and Given to Shame. this Pride observing inly Grievd. but knew not that. the rest was Givn to Shame as well as this. Then Nineva & Babylon & Costly tyre. And evn Jerusalem was Shewn. the holy City. Then Athens Learning & the Pride of Greece. and further from the Rising Sun. was Rome Seated on Seven hills the mistress of the world. Emblem of Pride She Saw the Arts their treasures Bring and luxury his bounteous table Spread. but now a Cloud oercasts. and back to th'East. to Constan- tines Great City Empire fled, Ere long to bleed & die a Sacrifice done by a Priestly hand[.] So once the Sun his. Chariot drew. back. to prolong a Good kings life.

The Cloud oer past & Rome now Shone again Miterd & Crown'd with triple crown. Then Pride was better Pleasd She Saw the World fall down in Adoration[.] But now full to the Setting Sun a Sun arose out of the Sea. it rose & shed Sweet Influence oer the Earth Pride feared for her City, but not long. for looking Stedfastly She saw that Pride Reignd here. Now Direful Pains accost her. and Still pregnant. so Envy came & Hate, twin progeny Envy hath a Serpents head

of fearful bulk hissing with hundred tongues, her poisnous
breath breeds Satire foul Contagion from which none are
free. oer whelmd by ever During Thirst She Swalloweth her
own Poison. which consumes her nether Parts. from
whence a River Springs. Most Black & loathsom through the
land it Runs Rolling with furious Noise. but at the last it
Settles in a lake called Oblivion. tis at this Rivers fount
where evry mortals Cup is Mix't My Cup is fill'd with Envy's
Rankest Draught a miracle No less can set me Right. Desire
Still pines but for one Cooling Drop and tis Deny'd. while
others in Contentments downy Nest do sleep, it is the
Cursed thorn wounding my breast that makes me sing. however sweet tis Envy that Inspires my Song. prickt. by the
fame of oters how I mourn and my complaints are Sweether
than their Joys but O could I at Envy Shake my hands. my
notes Should Rise to meet the New born Day. Hate Meager
hag Sets Envy on unable to Do ought herself. but Worn
away a Bloodless Daemon The Gods all Serve her at her will
so great her Power is[.] like. fabled hecate She doth bind
them of her law. Far in a Direful Cave She lives unseen
Closd from the Eye of Day, to the hard Rock transfixt by
fate and here She works her witcheries that when She
Groans She Shakes the Solid Ground Now Envy She controlls with her numming trance & Melancholy Sprung from
her dark womb There is a Melancholy, O how lovely tis
whose heaven is in the heavnly Mind for she from heaven
came, and where She goes heaven still doth follow her. She
brings true Joy once fled. & Contemplation is her Daughter.
Sweet Contemplation. She brings humility to man take her
She Says & wear her in thine heart lord of thy Self thou then
art lord of all. Tis Contemplation teacheth knowledge truly
how to know. and Reinstates him on his throne once lost
how lost I'll tell. But Stop the motley Song I'll Shew. how
Conscience Came from heaven. But O who listens to his
Voice. T'was Conscience who brought Melancholy down
Conscience was sent a Guard to Reason. Reason once fairer
than the light till fould in Knowledges dark Prison house.
For knowledge drove sweet Innocence away. and Reason
would have followd but fate sufferd not. Then down Came
Conscience with his lovely band The Eager Song Goes on
telling how Pride against her father Warrd & Overcame.

Down his white Beard the Silver torrents Roll. and Swelling
Sighs burst forth his Children all in arms appear to tear him
from his throne Black was the deed. most Black. Shame in
a Mist Sat Round his troubled head. & filld him with Confusion. Fear as a torrent wild Roard Round his throne the
mightly pillars shake Now all the Gods in blackning Ranks
appear. like a tempestuous thunder Cloud Pride leads. them
on. Now they Surround the God. and bind him fast. Pride
bound him, then usurpd oer all the Gods. She Rode upon
the Swelling wind and Scatterd all who durst t'oppose. but
Shame opposing fierce and hovering. over her in the dark-
ning Storm. She brought forth Rage. Shame bore honour &
made league with Pride. Mean while Strife Mighty Prince
was born Envy in direful Pains him bore. then Envy brought
forth Care. Care Sitteth in the wrinkled brow. Strife Shape-
less Sitteth under thrones of kings. like Smouldring fire. or
in the Buzz of Cities flies abroad Care brought forth Covet
Eyeless & prone to th'Earth, and Strife brought forth
Revenge. Hate brooding in her Dismal den grew Pregnant
& bore Scorn, & Slander. Scorn waits on Pride. but Slander.
flies around the World to do the Work of hate her drudge &
Elf. but Policy doth drudge for hate as well as Slander. &
oft makes use of her. Policy Son of Shame. Indeed hate
Controlls all the Gods. at will. Policy brought forth Guile &
fraud. these Gods last namd live in the Smoke of Cities. on
Dusky wing breathing forth Clamour & Destruction. alas in
Cities wheres the man whose face is not a mask unto his
heart Pride made a Goddess. fair or Image rather till
knowledge animated it. 'twas Calld Selflove. The Gods
admiring loaded her with Gifts as once Pandora She 'mongst
men was Sent. and worser ills attended her by far. She was
a Goddess Powerful & bore Conceit[.] & Policy doth dwell
with her by whom she [had] Mistrust & Suspition. Then
bore a Daughter called Emulation. who. married. honour
these follow her around the World[.] Go See the City friends
Joind Hand in Hand. Go See. the Natural tie of flesh &
blood. Go See more strong the ties of marriage love. thou
Scarce Shall find but Self love Stands Between

Much in this passage, such as Pride's visions or the praise
of Melancholy or the curse of Envy, does not involve kinship

metaphor. Much of the allegory that does involve kinship metaphor depends on other metaphors as well. There are forms of causation and creation and derivation here other than progeneration, as when Pride makes an image called Self-Love (this derives from *causation as direct manipulation,* discussed in chapter 4) or when the gods who live in the city breath forth clamour and destruction; one other case of breathing forth—when Envy's "poisnous breath breeds Satire"—relies only partially, coherently, on kinship metaphor, involving the *biological resource as parent* inference, wherein the parent can be simply the biological stuff and raw material used as source.

Nonetheless, kinship as metaphor is the principal domain underlying this exposition of human psychology. Though parts of the passage are obscure and some opaque, its intent and basic outline are clear. Pride has warred against her father. Though unnamed, the father is likely to be knowledge. The passage describing his dethronement is punctuated by an insertion concerning Conscience, Reason, and Knowledge which is set off linguistically from the genealogical allegory by the parenthetical phrases "But Stop the motley Song" and "The Eager Song Goes on." Connecting the text on either side of the parentheses suggests that it is knowledge who has lost his throne:

Tis Contemplation teacheth knowledge truly how to know.
and Reinstates him on his throne once lost how lost I'll tell.
But Stop the motley Song . . . The Eager Song Goes on telling how Pride against her father Warrd & Overcame. Down his white Beard the Silver torrents Roll. and Swelling Sighs burst forth his Children all in arms appear to tear him from his throne Black was the deed.

That Shame and Fear are the allies of Pride in the dethronement and that Blake explicitly states that the father sees "his Children all in arms" suggests that Pride, Shame, and Fear are the offspring of Knowledge. Certainly the text concerns principally the genealogies of Pride, Shame, and Fear. Its global intent is to show how the emotions or powers of psychology in these genealogies have ignored a kind of humility, dethroned knowledge, and raised up instead components of psychology like self-love. These replacements rend and interfere with actual kinship ties, natural ties of flesh and blood, and other ties such as friendship.

What are the genealogies of Fear, Pride, and Shame? Fear produces both Pale Desire, who fathers Curiosity, a virgin, and Leaden Sloth, who produces Ignorance, who produces Wonder. Pride (somehow involving Shame?) produces Ambition; she also produces the twin sisters Envy and Hate. Envy is mother to Melancholy, who is mother to Contemplation. (Bentley indicates that in the original manuscript, a phrase calling Humility the daughter of Contemplation has been deleted.) Envy is mother to her son Strife, who produces Revenge, and mother to Care, who produces Covet. Hate is mother to Scorn and Slander. Shame produces Honor and is also mother to her son Policy, who produces Guile and Fraud. It is said that Shame makes league with Pride. Their genealogies combine: Pride fashions Self-Love, who produces Conceit and Emulation, who marries Honor, who is born of Shame. And Self-Love, made by Pride, mates with Policy, the son of Shame, to produce Mistrust and Suspicion. An alternative reading of the manuscript by Bentley (see appendix 3A) omits the marriage of Emulation and Honor and the birth of Mistrust.

Many metaphoric inferences work to weave this text together. *Behaves-as*, a special case of the *functional property transfer* inference pattern, appears often, as when Curiosity is made a young virgin, since there is a conceptual stereotype of young virgins behaving with curiosity. The *behaves-as* inference pattern let us understand both the revolt of Pride against Knowledge and the conflicts and alliances between the houses of Pride, Shame, and Fear. These powers conflict in ways we can see as analogous to conflicts stereotypically attached to the child-father and sibling-sibling relations. A dovetailing of *constraint of kinship term* and *property transfer* occurs when Policy—that is, political cunning—is made a son, since social and certainly political activity are stereotypically male, as I discuss in chapter 2. Envy and Hate are *grouped* because of their *similarity* as two avatars of the same aspect of psychology.

The dominant metaphoric inference is *lineage*: the text relies principally on the generation of a feeling or a behavior from a parent feeling or behavior. Fear, a combination of dread and reverence and of the resultant avoidance and attraction, produces two sets of progeny. (1) Principally out of avoidance and distance comes sloth. Slothfulness, distance, and disengagement can lead to ignorance. And since there is wonder at things we are ignorant of, wonder is the progeny of ignorance. (2) Principally out of reverence and attraction comes a kind of desire, not the desire of love or lust, but the desire for those things that we fear and do not know: pale desire. Curiosity stems from it since we can be curious only where we are distanced. Curiosity requires strangeness in the thing regarded (hence the characterization of Curiosity as a virgin, who both desires and fears). The genealogy is subtle: Wonder and Curiosity share a common ancestor. They, like Ignorance, Sloth, and Pale Desire, all have an element of separation from the objects they regard, and the element of fear in each of them keeps them non-aggressive. No burning desire or possessiveness or belligerency or manipulative analysis stems from fear, but there are kinds of interest and distance that do, and Blake's genealogy, far from the casual product of a fevered visionary, shrewdly relates them.

That Pride should result in Ambition for oneself and in Envy of others is clear. Envy and Hatred are twins because they stem from the same displeasure at another's success. Failed ambition particularly results in envy and hatred, and failure, producing despondency, engenders Melancholy. As a state of inactivity and introspection, Melancholy can, with some assistance from *inheritance*, produce Contemplation. And introspection into one's failure can, with some assistance from Heaven, lead to Humility.

It is no surprise, then, that one feeling—Pride—can lead to its contrary—Humility. Pride can initiate a process of experience that ultimately leads to humility: this is a frequent stereotype of adolescence and young adulthood and a popular theme in didactic literature. It is all the more fitting in Blake that pride can lead to humility since Blake's concept of humility is not that it is antithetical to pride but rather a tool toward accomplishing Pride's very goal: if you have humility, you are "lord of thyself," and "thou then art lord of all." Shame also can produce Honor, for knowledge of Shame can produce guilt and produce desire for purification through belief and action: the world's religions rely heavily on this psychological process. The passage also suggests that the concept of shame makes the concept of honor possible.

Conflicting feelings can have the same progenitor, and this highlights a crucial point: we hold not one stereotype of human mental operation but many stereotypes, one for each potential process, and these potentialities are often opposed alternatives. Thus Pride can result in either Melancholy or Rage, and this is no surprise. Pride plus a feeling of failure and inadequacy can bring Melancholy. Pride plus thwarted Ambition and redoubled self-assertion can bring Rage.

One feeling can have many different offspring down the tree of its progeny. Pride produces twin sisters Hate and Envy. Envy, born of Pride, can produce Strife between envier and envied and desire by the envier for whatever the envied possesses. Strife, born of Envy, promotes both Revenge on the envied and Covetousness of what the envied possesses. Yet Hate, equally born of Pride, results not in Covetousness of things or Revenge on the envied but rather in Scorn and Slander. Why this difference between the offspring of the twin sisters Hate and Envy? First, Hate is a more broken state than Envy; there is less will to succeed in it. So Scorn *inherits* the weakness, but Revenge *inherits* the willfulness. Second, prideful Envy is directed at only those who are enviable, whereas prideful Hate can be directed at anybody, including manifest inferiors.

Let us pursue the genealogies of Pride, Shame, and Fear. Neither a Fear that is distanced but interested nor a self-concerned Pride engenders political cunning, but rather Shame produces scurrilous Policy, something both feeling and behavior, with its two offspring behaviors Guile and Fraud.

That Pride should create Self-Love and that Self-Love should engender Conceit require no explanation, but that Self-Love should engender Emulation does. Though "emulation" now implies principally the imitation of others to better oneself, and though it has had this as one of its senses as far back as the sixteenth century this sense was once balanced by now-obsolete negative senses of "emulation," in which "to emulate" could mean "to be jealous of, envy, feel a grudge against" and "emulation" could mean "ambitious rivalry for power or honours; contention or ill-will between rivals" and "grudge against the superiority of others; dislike, or tendency to disparagement, of those who are superior." These negative senses follow easily from self-love, but self-love need not imply blind megalomania: self-love combined with respect for another can motivate virtuous Emulation, and it is this Emulation who marries Honor. Thus again, we hold more than one stereotype as a potential. Self-love can produce either blind, self-praising conceit or less self-praising emulation. Conceit and Emulation oppose each other, though behavior may alternate between them, just as the same Pride may stand behind behavior alternating between Rage and Melancholy.

It is the union of a high regard for oneself (Self-Love) and a shameful approach to others (Policy) that accounts for Mistrust and Suspicion of others, and we understand this by reference to progenerative coupling: the coupling of Self-Love and Policy generates Mistrust and Suspicion.

Before leaving Blake's elaborate genealogy of mental states, I should note again that since we conceive of mental events as resulting from either single or multiple preceding events, the stereotype of kinship must be modified when it is used extensively and in detail as a metaphor for *lineage* in the world, mind, and behavior. The requirement for double parentage must be explained away. Milton and Hesiod represent offspring as born from the brow. Blake's alternative proposal is to state that "Gods like these nor male nor female are but Single Pregnate, or, if they list, together mingling bring forth mighty powers."

Human condition: Psychology and behavior in
Spenser's Medina, Perissa, and Elissa

Like Blake, Spenser uses kinship metaphor to express the relationships between certain feelings and behaviors, but *The Faerie Queene* does so with much less elaboration of the kinship tree, restricting itself to parents and their immediate offspring. In particular, Spenser has a fondness for using *inheritance* and idealized cognitive models of sibling relationships to help him present the relations between certain behaviors. In book 2, canto 2, for example, three daughters share one father, but each has a different mother. Each of the three sisters is a disposition of character; herein they share an *inheritance* from their father, who can be taken allegorically as mind. But insofar as each has a different mother, each inherits a qualitatively different disposition: the eldest, Elissa, is haughty, proud, reserved, severe. The youngest, Perissa, practises pleasure and delight and laughter and lightness. The middle sister, Medina, represents an Aristotelian golden mean. Here, double parentage as an aspect of kinship is used by Spenser to convey his sense of relation between the three behaviors. He therefore highlights the double parentage: a common father accounts for *inherited similarity;* the different mothers account for *inherited* differences.

The gradient of eldest, middle, and youngest is used as a metaphor for a gradient of behavior: the middle mediates opposed polar excesses. Each sister has a suitor or companion: Elissa has proud and reserved, almost puritanical Huddibras; Perissa has lawless Sans-loy; and Medina has temperate Guyon. Huddibras and Sans-loy, excessive themselves and goaded on by the excessive sisters whom they serve, battle each other. Temperate Guyon seeks to pacify them, but the intercession of Medina is required before the pacification succeeds. By her temperance and balance, she ultimately brings whatever is excessive under the sway of measure and propriety. To confirm and bind their league, Medina then leads the combatants in to dine. In both passages, we see Medina constantly operating to rein in the excesses embodied in her sisters (see appendices 3B and 3C).

Kinship metaphor underlies the *inheritance* and partially underlies the oppositional balanced symmetry of eldest-middle-youngest at work in this text. But the idea that the middle rules and reconciles the oldest and youngest comes from the allegory and is not required by connotations of kinship. Indeed, stereotypes of behavior attached to kinship terms can alternatively indicate that the eldest rules. And stereotypes drawn from folktales can alternatively indicate that the youngest of three sisters or brothers is the good one, the most sublime example being Cordelia in *King Lear*.

Human condition: Psychology, behavior, personality
development, and biological generation in Spenser's
Belphoebe and Amoretta

The use of sibling relations to indicate that one essence
has taken two avatars—seen before in Milton's Sin and Death
and more briefly and clearly in Blake's twins Envy and
Hate—can be found in book 3, canto 6 of *The Faerie Queene*.
Belphoebe and Amoretta, twins by virgin birth, embody a
mutual inheritance of grace, femininity, beauty, virtue:

> Her mother was the faire Chrysogonee,
> The daughter of Amphisa, who by race
> A Faerie was, yborne of high degree,
> She bore Belphoebe, she bore in like cace
> Faire Amoretta in the second place:
> *These two were twinnes, and twixt them two did share*
> *The heritage of all celestiall grace.*
> *That all the rest it seem'd they robbed bare*
> *Of bountie, and of beautie, and all vertues rare.*

At their birth, one is taken by Phoebe (Artemis) and the
other by Venus (Aphrodite) to rear, and thus their femininity
and its essential grace and virtue, commonly held at birth,
assume two different expressions:

> Vp they them tooke, each one a babe vptooke,
> And with them carried, to be fostered;
> Dame Phoebe to a Nymph her babe betooke,
> To be vpbrought in perfect Maydenhed,
> And of her selfe her name Belphoebe red:
> But Venus hers thence farre away conuayd,
> To be vpbrought in goodly womanhed,
> And in her litle loues stead, which was strayed,
> Her Amoretta cald, to comfort her dismayd.

Virtuous and beautiful femininity, an identical *inheritance* of
twins, takes its two different expressions in maidenhood and
womanhood and the different behaviors stereotypically
attached to those concepts.

The birth of Belphoebe and Amoretta depends upon the
metaphoric inference of *biological resource as parent*, discussed in chapter 2, wherein the sheer stuff of the universe,
such as earth and water and atmosphere, can be considered

the progenitor. In a long passage, Spenser explains the fathering by the sun of Belphoebe and Amoretta upon Chrysogone. It is a miniature and easily accessible exploration of *biological resource as parent* as manifest in a particular "straunge ensample of conception" (see appendix 3D).

Human condition: Psychology and behavior in Spenser's Priamond, Diamond, and Triamond

The most precise use of *inheritance* as a partitioning of attributes is Spenser's tale of Priamond, Diamond, and Triamond in book 4, canto 2. Triplets of one knight, they do not know their father, but they explicitly *inherit* a partitioning of his qualities. Spenser divides the physical qualities of knightly combat into three sets of two complementary components each: stoutness and strength, foot and horse, spear and axe. All three brothers fight well, but each possesses a unique selection from these three sets of qualities. Each possesses all of one set, plus half of each of the other two sets. Triamond is both stout and strong; Priamond is stout but not so strong; Diamond is strong but not so stout. And so for the other two sets:

> Stout Priamond, but not so strong to strike,
> Strong Diamond, but not so stout a knight,
> But Triamond was stout and strong alike:
> On horsebacke vsed Triamond to fight,
> And Priamond on foote had more delight,
> But horse and foote knew Diamond to wield;
> With curtaxe vsed Diamond to smite,
> And Triamond to handle speare and shield,
> But speare and curtaxe both vsd Priamond in field.

Spenser is absolutely explicit about partitioning as *inheritance* which *groups* the siblings for their *inherited similarity*, but he differentiates them according to the boundaries of the partition. The three knights are different components of a progenerative one:

> These three did loue each other dearely well,
> And with so firme affection were allyde,
> As if but one soul in them all did dwell,
> Which did her powre into three parts diuyde;

Like three faire branches budding farre and wide,
That from one roote deriu'd their vitall sap:
And like that roote that doth her life diuide,
Their mother was, and had full blessed hap,
These three so noble babes to bring forth at one clap.

At the close of this passage, kinship metaphor and branching as a metaphor cohere and collude to represent the partitioning of a unity.

Cosmos texts: The universe in Hesiod

Kinship and cosmogony. The expression of cosmogony as the history of a family line, frequent throughout the ancient Near East, is most famously exemplified by Hesiod's *Theogony,* though other texts, such as Egyptian and Babylonian creation myths, would reveal equally well the remarkable fitness of kinship proliferation as a metaphor for the original unfolding of the universe.

How does kinship fit cosmogony? First, it accounts for newness, of both entities and qualities. An offspring is a *new entity*; it is neither of its preexisting parents, but rather a creation of something that did not exist before. And since an offspring is not an exact copy of a parent, it must have some *new qualities.* So genealogy is ready at hand to express the creation of newness of different types.

Second, a family proliferating from *few* to *many* can be used to capture the unfolding and multiplying in a universe. Family proliferation can even be the unfolding of one into many under some models of conception, such as those where double parentage is not required (as when individuals can be "single pregnate") or where the wind or rain can impregnate. So kinship at once can explain the division of unity (one parent) or the progenerative coupling of two components of reality (two parents) to create other components of reality.

Third, an offspring *inherits* qualities from its parent(s). Thus family resemblance can be used to explain similarities that run throughout a group of cosmic aspects.

Fourth, some components of an offspring are seen as neither strictly copied nor new but rather as manifestations of qualities latent in parents, as highlightings, or as elaborations, or as blendings, or as any of the other results that we see derived from sexual genetics but for which we have no accurate common word, simply because there are too many such results. They all fade into each other without sharp distinction. We group them under a concept of family resemblance but do not seem to be able to resolve them into a a finite set of discrete primitives.

Fifth, sympathies and hostilities between family members—and between factions of family members, as determined by level of generation, sex, dependency relations, and self-interest—can be used to explain dynamic forces and alliances and conflicts and tensions in the cosmos.

In a nutshell, an offspring, a new thing, is, all at once, the same as, similar to, a manifestation of, a development of, a specification of, a difference from, and a conflict with its parents. *This captures creation of things and qualities, and the universal structure of sameness and difference.*

One coherent set of metaphoric inferences in particular finds repeated use in the explanation of cosmogony as generational succession: offspring *inherit* aspects of a parent, and these aspects are sometimes a partition of the parent taken holistically, as if the general concept could be resolved into elements. This elements are sometimes the components that the parent comprises, sometimes manifestations of a concept not seen except in these manifestations, sometimes an application of a concept to a particular domain, and sometimes an avatar or role assumed by the concept in a particular realm of the cosmos; but these uses all cohere, and the lines between them blur.

The Theogony. The family in the *Theogony* is extraordinarily profuse, and much of it will pass without mention here, either because the offspring are not aspects of the cosmos—as when the genealogy descends to explanation of particular heroes and nymphs or to the etiology of very local phenomena—or because the genealogy has become merely schematic. Questions of historical precedents and analogues—such as whether the three fates correspond to triple aspects of a moon divinity—are not at issue. Rather, the concern is how a reader (or auditor) uses the kinship metaphor given him to understand the system which the poet endeavors to present.

The focus here will be principally the offspring of Chaos and secondarily what Hesiod calls (ll. 44-45) the "reverend race of gods whom Gaia (Earth) and wide Ouranos (Heaven) bore in the beginning" (θεῶν γένος αἰδοῖον πρῶτον κλείουσιν ἀοιδῇ ἐξ ἀρχῆς, οὓς Γαῖα καὶ Οὐρανὸς εὐρὺς ἔτικτεν). These lineages comprise most major aspects of the cosmos. Of less interest will be the particular progeny of Zeus as father of gods and men (θεῶν πατέρ' ἠδὲ καὶ ἀνδρῶν, l. 47).

The aspects of inheritance in the Theogony. In her *Genealogie als mythische Form: Studien zur Theogonie des Hesiod* (1936), Paula Philippson has strongly stressed the *inheritance* inference of kinship metaphor as underlying the *Theogony*: the cosmos is a great One which consists of the unfolding of the essence of the first ancestor (see appendix 3E for original):

The first ancestor survives in all its descendents. The original Being, which is inherent in the ancestor, is *an sich* timeless; it is not extinguished with the death of the ancestor, but rather appears in the ancestor's descendents successively, in ever renewed modification.

The form in which the *Genos* is portrayed is genealogy. . . so from this manifestation in the form of genealogy, we may conclude that the cosmos unfolds itself as a single, uniform, timeless Being into manifold modifications, in which this timeless Being is immanent.

All the appearances, forces, and laws of the cosmos form a *genos*-like oneness.

This account seems to me flawed in a way that is extraneous to the analysis at hand, a way that might be characterized as a kind of Hegelianism: Philippson explains both the order imposed on cosmic plurality and the mechanisms presented as accounting for the generation of cosmic diversity as a transcendent One unfolding its essence. But the text does not *require* the reader to infer the existence of the transcendent One. Philippson's view also fails to account for generation of offspring contrary to their parents—such as Day and Aither progenerated by the union of Night and Erebos—unless one imports the postulate that essences contain contraries.

Philippson correctly stresses the repeated use in the *Theogony* of progeneration as metaphor for the partitioning of attributes and for the *inheritance* of partitioned attributes by offspring.

Inheritance in Hesiodic cosmogony folds together with the *components* inference: the relatively local *components* of some embracing cosmic concept can simultaneously be discrete or highlighted attributes latent in the concept and *inherited* by the components. We might speak of *inheritance by specification* in cases of such highlighting, and, as a subcategory, of *inheritance by partition* where the specific manifestations exhaust the larger concept. (*Inheritance by partition* is often only suggested by a series that trails off.) For example, in Hesiod Earth is said to be the single parent of various geographical components, specifically the hills and the Pontos: γείνατο δ' Οὔρεα μακρά . . . ἥ δὲ καὶ ἀτρύγετον πέλαγος τέκεν, οἴδματι θυῖον, / Πόντον, ἄτερ φιλότητος ἐφιμέρου (ll. 129-32). Similarly, Dawn (Eos or Erigenia) brings forth Eosphorus (Dawn-bringer), and the gleaming stars with which heaven is crowned (ll. 381-82).

Inheritance/components underlies Hesiod's casting of the various qualities or aspects of water as the fifty daughters of Nereus and Doris, son of Pontos and daughter of Okeanos (l. 240). These aspects are not quite so recognizably the *components* of Pontos and Okeanos in the way that the long hills are components of Earth, but the process is similar. And certainly they are a partition of the attributes of Ocean and Sea, manifestations of the qualities latent in a larger concept of bodies of water, an *inheritance* by specification, much as the seven deadly sins *inherit* specific qualities from Sin and Death and ultimately from Satan. Pontos and Okeanos, males, cannot mate, so there is an intermediary step in which Pontos produces a son and Okeanos a daughter. These two in turn produce water-nymphs such as Galene (Calm), Cymothoe (the Wave-swift), Pherusa (She who speeds [ships]), Dynamene (She who has power), Cymodoce (the Wave-receiver), and Cymatolege (the Wave-stiller). The son of Pontos (Sea), called Nereus, seems to have *inherited* the sense of the sea as calm and deep and truthful. It is said that Nereus, the eldest of the children of Pontos, is true and does not lie, and that men call him the Old Man because he is

trusty and gentle and does not forget the laws of righteous-
ness, but thinks just and kindly thoughts (ll. 232-36). One of
the fifty daughters is said explicitly to have inherited the
qualities of her father: Νημερτής θ᾽ , ἤ πατρὸς ἔχει νοον
ἀθανάτοιο (l. 262). Her name, "Nemertes," means "the
Unerring" or "Truthful."

The *Theogony* is in fact rife with instances where the
offspring are the *components* of some generalized concept,
such as bodies of water, and are simultaneously seen as having *inherited* specific qualities of the generalized concept.
Hyperion and Theia, male and female Titans who seem to
have the qualities of bright daylight in general, give birth by
their union to Helios (Sun), Selene (Moon), and Eos (Dawn)
(ll. 371-74). Okeanos and Tethys, male and female Titans
who seem to have the qualities of water in general, give birth
by their union to various water-nymphs who have the specific
qualities of the rivers of their residence: Xanthe is the
"Brown" or "Turbid," Amphirho is the "Surrounding" river,
Ianthe is "She who delights," and Ocyrrhoe is the "Swift-
flowing." Other of these nymphs take their names from the
lands over which their rivers preside, as Europa, Asia, Doris,
Ianeira. If Okeanos and Tethys represent not water in general but specifically ocean, then these offspring must be taken
not as manifestations but as extensions.

Zeus as impregnating power and syncretizing Olympian
often unites with goddesses or nymphs or women, some of
whom derive from deities in non-Olympian myths, and the
quality of the female is partitioned into offspring who *inherit*
these manifestations. Zeus unites with Mnemosyne
(Eurybia), a Titan, who has the quality of memory, to produce the nine muses. The partitioned qualities of artistic
production are manifested in these muses (l. 75), much as
the partitioned qualities of knightly combat are manifested
in Priamond, Diamond, and Triamond. Zeus and
Eurynome produce the three Graces (ll. 907-8), Eurynome
having *inherited* her own grace from the gracefulness of the
waves, her father having been Okeanos. Zeus and Themis, a
Titan connected with the planets and hence with the order
and justice of the universe, produce (1) the Horae (Hours),
Eunomia (Order), Dike (Justice), and blooming Eirene
(Peace), who mind the works of moral men, and (2) the

Moerae (Fates) Klotho, and Lachesis, and Atropos, on whom Zeus bestowed the great honor of dispensing evil and good to mortal men (ll. 901-6). Zeus and Metis, who has the general quality of thought, produce Athena, the wisest of the goddesses, though Zeus first swallows Metis, and Athena must be born out of the head of Zeus.

A more complicated example of *inheritance by specification*, an example involving a blending of qualities, begins when Eurybia and Krius, Titans with the general sense of memory and mind, produce what seem to be three sons known for their wisdom, Astraeus, Pallas, and Perses. This is *inheritance*. Pallas then unites with Styx—a daughter of Okeanos and Tethys. She not only has *inherited* the power of the ocean but also was the first to come to the aid of Zeus against the Titans, for which Zeus gave her a much greater power over men and gods. This union produces offspring whose qualities at once *blend* and *specify* qualities of the parents. The offspring are Zelus (Valor), Nike (Victory), Kratos (Strength), and Bia (Force).

The genealogy of Gaia in Hesiod. The two major and disjoint genealogies in the *Theogony* are the lineages of Gaia (Earth) and of Chaos. In the first, Gaia bears starry Ouranos (Heaven), equal to herself, to cover her on every side (ll. 126-27). It is hard to conceive of this generation, chronologically the first in the lineage of Gaia and certainly the most important for understanding the structure of the visible cosmos, as in any way an unfolding of the essence of a first ancestor. For this reason I think Philippson's analysis, given earlier, is incomplete. Rather, this generation typifies the creation of many from one by division or separation of some original unity, a mechanism exemplified throughout ancient Near Eastern and Presocratic texts, as in Marduk's splitting of Tiamat into two equal parts to create the sky in the *Enuma Elish,* or the various Milesian accounts of the origin of the cosmos out of an *arche,* or the Pythagorean explanation of the generation of number (and hence the universe) by separation of an original unity according to the procedure of the gnomon. In various special cases of such generation, Earth bears sky as her cover, and here several metaphoric inferences of kinship terms cohere. The first is *biological resource as parent*, which, as explained in chapter 2, underlies those generations where the raw stuff of the cosmos needed to produce something is called the parent of the thing. *Biological resource as parent* underlies the generation of Ouranos to the extent that we conceive of it as a separating off of part of Gaia, as in the Tiamat myth. Second, *place and time as parent* applies to the generation of Ouranos in so far as primitive Earth was both the place and the time that produced Ouranos. The *order and succession* inference makes subsequent Ouranos the child of preceding Gaia. *Inheritance* has its place in so far as Ouranos is, like its parent, a component of the visible cosmos and of equal extent, making them structurally a matched pair.

This symmetry between Gaia and Ouranos and the covering of Gaia by Ouranos permit them to be characterized as woman and man coupling in the sense that, positionally, Ouranos and Gaia *behave* toward one another as man to woman in coition. Gaia and Ouranos produce Kronos. Kronos and Rhea produce Zeus. The violent transfer of rule from Ouranos to Kronos to Zeus—with Kronos encouraged by his mother Gaia to conquer his father Ouranos, and with Rhea saving her son Zeus from his father Kronos and thus permitting Zeus to overcome Kronos and become high ruler of the cosmos—evokes the *functional property transfer* inference pattern, since we understand the attitudes and behaviors here through stereotypes of kin standing in the named relations.

From the progenerative coupling of Gaia and Ouranos come twelve Titans, who are a suggested *inheritance by partition*. They consist of six pairs of brother and sister: Okeanos and Tethys, who have attributes of the sea, Hyperion and Theia, who have attributes of the sun and bright heavenly planets, Krius and Mnemosyne (Eurybia), who have attributes of memory, Koeus and Phoebe, who have attributes of the moon, Kronos and Rhea, who have attributes of harvests, and Iapetus and Themis, who have attributes of planets, and hence of order and justice. With the exception of memory, these attributes are components of neither heaven nor earth alone, but rather qualities that arise out of their interaction, or entities that exist between heaven and earth and were created by their separation. They are *components* of the earth-heaven structure as a unit, so that *components, causation,* and *inheritance* all coherently underlie an understanding of their generation.

Components and *inheritance by specification* again combine when the progenerative coupling of Gaia (earth) and Ouranos (sky) produces the three Cyclopes, Brontes (Thunderer), Steropes (Lightener), and Arges (Vivid One).

At one point in this genealogy of Gaia, kinship metaphor must stretch hard: two of the Titan offspring of Gaia and Ouranos have attributes of memory. How can memory spring from earth and heaven? Suppose one has the model that cosmic history, and certainly the history of the locale you can see, begins with the separation of heaven from earth. Then this separation creates history, man, and the arena of human concern and memory. So memory can spring from earth and heaven.

The genealogy of Chaos in Hesiod. The *inheritance* inference—and the sense that offspring recursively unfold a founding principle to make manifest its latent attributes and partition into specifics its general potentiality—underlies comprehensively any understanding of the elaborate, fascinating progeny of Chaos.

Chaos by itself generates Nux (Night) and Erebos (l. 123), female and male manifestations of darkness and heirs of the attributes of Chaos. The progenerative coupling of Nux and Erebos produces Hemera (Day) and Aither, the bright, untainted upper atmosphere, as distinguished from Aer, the lower atmosphere of the earth. These generations are understood as a coherence of *place and time as parent* and *order and succession*: the Night, as a place and time, produces Day; one gives way to the other in succession, comes out of the other. Since Chaos, Night, and Darkness are understood as initial conditions, Day and Aither must be subsequent to them—a frequent characterization familiar from Genesis—and hence Day and Aither are the offspring of Night and Erebos under *order and succession*. This generation, which does not seem to be an unfolding of a first principle, resembles a case in the *Enuma Elish*, where the progenerative coupling of Apsu and Tiamat, who have attributes of water, generates the male-female pair Lahmu and Lahamu, who have attributes of silt. First was the water, then the subsequent emergence of silt, which is therefore characterized as the offspring of water.

Inheritance/components unfolds a string of interrelated concepts mothered by Night, some of whom perhaps have Erebos as father (see ll. 209-32). They are Moros (Doom), Ker (Black Fate), Thanatos (Death), Hypnos (Sleep), To Phylon Oneiron (the Tribe of Dreams), Momos (Blame, Disgrace), Oizus (Painful Woe, Distress), Moirai and Kerai (the Destinies and ruthless avenging Fates, who are three: Klotho, who spins the thread of a man's life, Lachesis, who assigns to each man his destiny, and Atropos, who cuts the thread), Nemesis (the goddess of Retribution and Vengeance, usually by the gods), Apate (Cheating, Trickery, Fraud, Guile, Deceit), Philotes (Love, Affection), Geras (hateful Age), and Eris (hard-hearted Strife).

Note that the Fates are alternatively daughters both of Zeus and Themis (l. 904) and of Night (l. 217). This shows that one domain, like kinship, can offer perhaps many different metaphors for understanding a given concept. In one sense, fate is the child of Zeus, who is father of gods and men. In another sense, fate is the child of night.

Inheritance/components in turn unfolds Abhorred Strife into its children Ponos (painful Toil), Lethe (Forgetfulness), Limos (Hunger, Famine), Algea (tearful Sorrows, Pains), Hysmine (Fight), Mache (Battle), Phonos (Murder), Androktasia (Manslaughter), Neikos (Quarrel), Pseudes (Lie), Amphilogia (Dispute), Dysnomia (Lawlessness), and Ate (Ruin, Mischief). These offspring are said to be all of one nature (l. 230).

(There is, incidentally, a similar partitioning of the aspects of chaos and darkness in an Egyptian cosmogony, which lists, prior to creation, eight gods of chaos, "a god and a goddess for each quality of chaos. . . . These four pairs of gods persisted in mythology as the 'Eight' who were before the beginning. They were Nun, the primordial waters, and his consort Naunet, who came to be the counterheaven; Huh, the boundless stretches of primordial formlessness, and his consort Hauhet; Kuk, 'darkness', and his consort Kauket; and Amun, that is Amon, 'the hidden', representing the intangibility and imperceptibility of chaos, with his consort,

Amaunet" [Wilson 1974, p. 61]. Thereafter come the nine gods comprised of Atum with the eight derived from him, together known as the Ennead, who are divinities of progressive order in contrast to the eight divinities of chaos. These gods of order versus gods of Chaos resemble Hesiod's genealogy of Gaia versus the genealogy of Chaos, particularly since the Egyptian gods of order also include Earth and Sky [Geb and Nut], who beget the beings that populate the universe.)

Sleep and the Tribe of Dreams occur stereotypically during Night and hence are its offspring under *place and time as parent*. It might be said that the temporal connection of Love with night accounts for its generation under *place and time as parent*, except that Philotes can have connotations of affection rather than eros.

All the members of the first generation of Night's offspring, including Sleep and Dream and Affection, are *grouped* because the are *similar* to the extent that each is a manifestation of the powers of Night and Darkness: death and blame and woe and doom and fate and the destinies and the others all work darkly against the order invented by men, bring an irrational power to bear on him (this accounts for Philotes), or limit his existence. Similarly, all the offspring of Strife, excepting Oath, are *components* and *inherited specifications* of the powers of Chaos and Darkness, setting men at odds with each other, with the cosmos, with wisdom, memory, knowledge, peace, pleasure, and institutional and rational order. These *components* are *grouped* as offspring because of *similar inheritance*. Oath is both a consequence of Strife—since it is the existence of Strife (and Lie and Deceit) that makes Oath necessary—and a form of Strife itself, since it troubles men deeply and puts them at odds with contentment.

These manifestations, specifications, and elaborations of the general potentialities of Chaos, Darkness, and the irrational all oppose, as a family, the family of natural order derived from Gaia and Ouranos. Specifically, the Titan attributes of light (sun and moon and dawn) are set against darkness; memory is set against forgetfulness; harvests are set against famine; justice is set against lawlessness; and even the attributes of the sea, which, it will be remembered, has been described as fundamentally graceful and truthful, are set against lies and toil and strife in general. Chaos in general is set against the earth-heaven unit in general, and the two disjoint genealogies are understood mainly, though with clear exceptions, by reference to our stereotypes of *inheritance* in parent-child relations. (The reader interested in this kind of differentiation of Chaos will find some comments on Ovid in appendix 3F.)

Cosmos: Chaos and Night as the enemies of order

Gower, Spenser, and Milton, probably influenced by Hesiod, Ovid, or Heracleitus, set a family of Chaos and Night in opposition to the God or gods of order. Chaos in these passages is the raw stuff out of which order is built, as it is in the first twenty lines of Ovid's *Metamorphoses,* where it is said to contain warring seeds. This is *biological resource as parent* since the raw cosmic stuff needed to produce something is called the parent of what is produced.

Milton's passage (*Paradise Lost* 2.890-917; see appendix 3G) calls Chaos and Night "Ancestors of Nature." Night and Chaos hold "Eternal Anarchy" over "hold, cold, moist, and dry," the stuff of generation. *Place and time as parent* assists to the extent that Chaos is conceived dimly as a place and the era of world-forming as a time. So Milton can call "this wild Abyss / The Womb of nature."

Spenser's passage (*Faerie Queene* 3.6.36-37; see appendix 3H) calls Chaos "the wide wombe of the world" because it "supplyes / the substances of natures fruitfull progenyes." This is the clearest example of a case where *biological resource as parent* underlies the transformation of cosmic stuff into life. Spenser states explicitly that the "substance is eterne, and bideth so," but that when the stuff is endowed with form and feature, it "Becomes a bodie, and doth then inuade / The state of life." Upon death, form leaves, but the stuff persists: "Ne when the life decayse, and forme does fade, doth it consume."

In Gower's passage (*Mirour de l'Omme*, ll. 49-72; see appendix 3I), Nothingness in some obscure sense gives birth to Sin. This may snag you, since you saw Satan give birth to

Sin in Gower, but in the realm of metaphor, identity is not necessarily exclusive, or symmetric, or transitive. In different metaphors that focus on different, overlapping, or even the same aspects of Sin, Sin might have many different genealogies, and this does not imply that any two of them are equal.

In the Gower passage, Sin is never explicitly called the offspring of Nothingness, but Nothingness is said to contain sin, indeed to be sin, and sin is personified as an agent. Gower, like the other authors considered, sets the powers of darkness against the God who creates order. Nothingness, says Gower, was created before God and without him. He cites John the apostle as his source for this, probably the line καὶ χωρὶς αὐτοῦ ἐγένετο οὐδὲ ἕν, or "Omnia per ipsum facta sunt: et sine ipso factum est nihil, quod factum est. In ipso vita erat" (John 1:3), usually punctuated and translated to mean that "not anything was created without God" rather than that "Nothingness was created without him."

Sin in this passage simultaneously is Nothingness, is contained as the sole *component* of Nothingness ("nothingness contains in itself only the name of sin"), and *inherits* from Nothingness its power and desire to annihilate, particularly to annihilate the works of God ("for sin annihilates all good"). It also *behaves* as an offspring in so far as it is loyal to its progenitor and works as his agent, a behavior we have already seen Gower ascribe to offspring considered as members of a feudal family power.

I find this an interesting case because the metaphor is only suggested. It is almost as if, just as a metaphor prompts and guides us in a search for inferences and models to use as tools of understanding, so the text here only suggests a direction in which to seek a metaphor which will in turn supply useful inferences and models. In this case, *inheritance*, *behaves-as*, and the various idealized cognitive models of kin are useful in building an understanding of the passage. Of course, other helpful routines of understanding might be found. One might assume that sin and Nothingness are identical and so not need *inheritance* to grasp their similarity. Even then, kinship metaphor might be applied as a reinforcement to that understanding.

Marriage as union and blending: John Redford and
Martianus Capella

In the passages considered so far, marriage has been used as the establishment of a progenerative couple. But allegories exist wherein marriage is a metaphor for union and blending. Since we have the conceptual metaphor that marriage is union, marriage can be used noncreatively to characterize union, giving the converse conceptual metaphor, that union is marriage. These allegories we understand by reference to *functional property transfer:* one thing pursuing another, desiring another, having difficulty attaining another, and so on, is *behavior* like the behavior in our idealized cognitive models of courtship. The blending or synthesis of things, the tension within a unity, the balance of qualities in a thing, and so on, is *behavior* or *functioning* like the behavior and functioning in our idealized cognitive models of marital union. Other inferences may amplify the understanding provided by this reference to *functional property transfer.*

The difference between marriage as progenerative coupling and marriage as union of two things is compendiously illustrated by a sixteenth century moral interlude by John Redford, *Wit and Science.* There are two marriages in the interlude, one before the story begins between husband Reason and wife Experience, and the second, the subject of the play, between their daughter Science (Knowledge) and her suitor Wit, who might be taken as youthful intelligence, studious and diligent, but as yet insufficiently instructed and, because lacking in experience, overconfident. The marriage of Reason and Experience is a progenerative coupling, motivated by the desire to illuminate the sources of Knowledge. It relies for its understanding on two parts of the inference indicating *lineage* in the world, mind, and behavior. That Reason is the father of Knowledge is an instance of Thought producing Knowledge; that Experience is the mother of Knowledge is an instance of the history of mental operations, as provoked by world situations, affecting Mind. The marriage of Reason and Experience is the uniting of (1) the power of the mind to change its internal state by operating on itself and (2) the power of the mind to change its internal state by processing information from world situations. These two powers work in complementary ways to produce knowledge; the marriage is a kind of united labor to affect knowledge—this much we understand by reference to *lineage*, and its usual supercategory inference, *causation*. Knowledge also has two different aspects: one, a kind of syllogistic and formal knowing, derives from Reason; the other, a kind of proverbial and aphoristic knowing, derives from Experience. One operates by processing and analyzing the matter at hand, the other by invoking the wisdom of tradition. Knowledge metaphorically *inherits* different but compatible qualities from her different but compatible parents.

The marriage of Wit and Science is not a progenerative coupling, like the marriage of Reason and Experience, but an attainment of one thing by another as a result of courtship. This species of marriage allegory we understand by reference to *functional property transfer*. Some of the potential stereotypical behaviors attached to participants in the courtship ritual are the desire of a young man for a young woman; the earned consent of the father that she be courted; the affection of the woman for the man; her bestowing of small favors and encouragements upon him; the attempt by the young man to accomplish certain tasks prerequisite to marriage; the loneliness and concern of the waiting lady whose beau is not treating her properly; the suspicion of the mother concerning the beau; the exchange of confidence from daughter to mother, and of advice from mother to daughter; the defense by the daughter against the suspicions of the mother; the waywardness of the young man, his neglect of propriety and ritual, his failure to accomplish what is prerequisite to marriage; his being repulsed by the young lady because of his bad behavior; his remorse at his behavior and resolution to perform properly; his shaming by the lady's father; the relenting of the father when he is convinced of the reformation of the young man, and his renewed consent to the courtship; the father's counsel that the daughter forego her emotional hurt and weigh the potential of the young man justly; the renewed efforts of the reformed young man to accomplish what is prerequisite to marriage; his success; the mutual love of the man and the woman; the consent to marriage; the marriage; the concern of the wife lest she be treated improperly during the marriage; the protestations of the young man that he will treat her properly, and why; the advising of the couple by the parents regarding the maintenance of proper marital behavior.

We bring to bear these stereotypical behaviors, and indeed many more specific behaviors of which these are generalizations, in understanding the courtship of Science by Wit.

Wit desires Lady Science. Reason, though with reservations, approves the courtship. Reason sets Wit the task of conquering Tediousness and indicates that Instruction should be his guide. Reason gives Wit a mirror in which he can see his true condition. Wit runs on ahead of Instruction, headstrong and overconfident. Though Study and Diligence fight for Wit, Tediousness wins. Wit loses his power and drive, and first seeks restoration with Lady Honest Recreation, but then reposes (his head) in the lap of (whore) Indolence, who amuses him with the stupidity of Ignorancy. Wit sleeps. Indolence trades the clothes of Ignorancy and Wit, so that Wit appears to be Ignorancy. Lady Science laments to her mother Experience that Wit has been so long from her. Experience suspects Wit's infidelity and insincerity and quotes proverbial wisdom to support her suspicions. Wit arrives, looks a fool and an ass, behaves abominably, wants a kiss, is told he is not the man he was, is repulsed. Wit looks into his mirror of Reason, realizes his state, feels remorse. Reason comes to shame him but relents when Wit sincerely pleads that he will reform. Now, listening to Instruction, Wit goes forth to conquer Tediousness with the help of Study and Diligence. The marriage is to ensue, but Wit must first counter the suspicions of the mother Experience and her daughter Science that he will fall from propriety after the marriage. With the help of Reason, he does so, and Wit attains Science.

Much of the stereotypical behavior invoked here as metaphor derives from the stereotype of the hero in folk tales: his initial failure at performing a task and the help of a donor before he ultimately succeeds. Other behavior invoked as metaphor derives not from kinship roles but other roles: Wit, Study, and Diligence fail the first time because they attack with brute strength; yet under the guidance of military tactician Instruction, they learn devious ways of fighting, and how to make "policy" succeed where "strength" fails. In all this, understanding proceeds by reference to stereotypical behaviors attached to holders of certain roles. Wit's general role is as potential husband, and hence the connection of his story with kinship metaphor; but he has a specialized role as heroic suitor of a noble lady, and another as military combatant. That these roles are compatible in our stereotypes permits the writer to ascribe behaviors from each of them to Wit, to use several types of behavioral metaphors at once, knowing that the metaphors will naturally cohere as the reader seeks to understand the text.

No doubt a more famous allegory of marriage, Martianus Capella's late Roman *De Nuptiis Philologiae et Mercurii* weds Philology to Mercury in a text of stultifying tediousness and superficial allegory. So, we began with Milton's brilliant use of the many cohering inferences of kinship metaphor in a compendious passage, and we end with Martianus Capella's reliance on elementary kinship metaphor to help his voluminous narrative limp along. This window on what commonly underlies them shows with what different levels of mastery the two authors wield the common resource.

Mercury, the god of eloquence, capable of deceit and speed, represents rhetoric. Philology, love of learning, and (insofar as Mercury is characterized as the logos) lover of Mercury, is to be his bride. Book 1 concerns their betrothal, book 2 their marriage, and the remaining seven books are the several speeches of the seven handmaidens presented to Philology: Grammar, Dialectic, Rhetoric, Geometry, Arithmetic, Astronomy, and Harmony. The last seven books constitute a school text on the seven liberal arts. This betrothal and wedding are a union of concepts rather than the establishment of a progenerative pair, but there are many other uses of kinship metaphor in the text that are straightforward and by now need no unpacking or illumination. Hymen, for instance, is pleased by dance because Bacchus is her father and sings at weddings because a Muse was her mother, both clear cases of *inheritance*. Hymen has the task of garlanding the thresholds blooming with flowers because the three Graces, who are said to be her kinsmen, have granted it to her, a clear case of Hymen being *treated-as* a kinsman. Wisdom is Philology's mother, a case of *inheritance*; and

Wisdom counsels Philology, a case of *treated-as* and *behaves-as*. And so on through the first two books.

In the story of the courtship and betrothal and wedding of Philology and Mercury which occupies the first two books, one over-flowing with superfluous detail, the metaphor runs away with the allegory. Consequently, much of the plot is motivated simply by the desire to present a wedding tale; it becomes a short novel, as it were, about a courtship, much of which has almost no connection with the allegory. Why, for instance, is it necessary in the *allegory* for Rhetoric to have the help of Juno? There is no reason. But in the *metaphor* of a courtship it makes predictable sense: Juno, as Jupiter's wife, can help persuade Jupiter to approve the betrothal of his son, Mercury, to a refined maiden who happens to be named Philology, and, as goddess of marriages, Juno's assistance is always helpful to a suitor. Some of the courtship metaphor does have allegorical significance, however, and its significance is, as in *Wit and Science,* the union of two things, a blending, a conjunction, a balance. Mercury, capable of deceit and trickery and disloyalty, all qualities with which rhetoric has been stigmatized since Plato, is obliged to show his sense of duty to superior powers, his sense of his place, and his devotion to Philology, the love of learning. Only then may he have Philology. Jupiter has explicitly delayed the marriage so that Mercury should not hasten into marriage on a youthful impulse and then, when he should have to go on his travels, lose something of his constancy. This reflects that a certain maturity is required before native dazzling intellect can take up the rigors of study properly and do learning justice. It is also said that Philology, who will not tolerate dozing off but requires wearisome vigils, will suit Mercury well since she can prevent him from becoming slothful and indolent, drowsy and languid. As in *Wit and Science,* this courtship, leading to a union of things, is understood by reference to *functional property transfer:* the two things, in their coming together, in the first stages of their potential union and blending, *behave* toward each other as man and maid; and in the projected stages of their developed union, they will complement, balance, and conflict as man and wife.

Conclusion

The lessons of this chapter are the lessons of this book displayed for one specific domain, literature. Human language relies on common mental systems shared by members of a linguistic community. It relies on shared basic metaphors, idealized cognitive models, and metaphoric inferences. Specifically, we seek to understand kinship metaphor in literature by finding common metaphoric inferences of kinship terms to guide us in metaphoric mappings; and those mappings involve idealized cognitive models of kin relations. What is common underlies what is exceptional, compelling, and deviant. What is common is the first and by far the most important step in understanding whatever is elite. The understanding of extended similes in literature is a hypertrophy of our capabilities for understanding conceptual metaphor.

APPENDIX

Appendix 3A

Bentley's (1978) alternative reading of the end of Blake's manuscript:

The Gods admiring loaded her with Gifts as once Pandora[.] She 'mongst men was Sent, and worser ills attended her by far. She was Goddess Powerful & bore Conceit & Emulation & Policy doth dwell with her by Whom She had a Son Called suspition[.] Go See the City[,] friends Join'd Hand in Hand. Go See the Natural tie of flesh & blood. Go See more strong the ties of marriage love, thou Scarce Shall find but Self love Stands Between[.]

Bentley's text also indicates that a phrase calling humility the daughter of contemplation is deleted in the manuscript.

Appendix 3B

Medina's mediation at battle:

> Her gracious wordes their rancour did appall,
> And suncke so deepe into their boyling brests,
> That downe they let their cruell weapons fall,
> And lowly did abase their loftie crests
> To her fair presence, and discrete behests.
> Then she began a treatie to procure,
> And stablish termes betwixt both their requests,
> That as a law for euer should endure;
> Which to obserue in word of knights they did assure.

Appendix 3C

Medina's mediation at the table:

> And those two froward sisters, their faire loues
> Came with them eke, all were they wondrous loth,
> And fained cheare, as for the time behoues,
> But could not colour yet so well the troth,
> But that their natures bad appeard in both:
> For both did at their second sister grutch,
> And inly grieue, as doth an hidden moth
> The inner garment fret, not th'vtter touch;
> One thought their cheare too litle, th'other thought too
> mutch.

> Elissa (so the eldest hight) did deeme
> Such entertainment base, ne ought would eat,
> Ne ought would speake, but euermore did seeme
> As discontent for want of merth or meat;
> No solace could her Paramour intreat
> Her once to show, ne court, nor dalliance,
> But with bent lowring browes, as she would threat,
> She scould, and frownd with froward countenaunce,
> Vnworthy of fair Ladies comely gouernaunce.

> But young Perissa was of other mind,
> Full of disport, still laughing, loosely light,
> And quite contrary to her sisters kind;
> No measure in her mood, no rule of right,
> But poured out in pleasure and delight;
> In wine and meats she flowd aboue the bancke,

And in excesse exceeded her owne might;
In sumptuous tire she ioyd her selfe to prancke,
But of her loue too lauish (little haue she thancke.)

Fast by her side did sit the bold Sans-loy,
Fit mate for such a mincing mineon,
Who in her loosenesse tooke exceeding ioy;
Might not be found a franker franion,
Of her lewd parts to make companion;
But Huddibras, more like a Malecontent,
Did see and grieue at his bold fashion;
hardly could he endure his hardiment,
Yet still he sat, and inly did him selfe torment.

Betwixt them both the faire Medina sate
With sober grace, and goodly carriage:
With equall measure she did moderate
The strong extremities of their outrage;
That forward paire she euer would asswage,
When they would striue dew reason to exceed;
But that some froward twaine would accourage,
And of her plenty adde vnto their need:
So kept she them in order, and her selfe in heed.

Appendix 3D

Biological resource as parent in Spenser: the sun, Chrysogone, Amoretta, and Belphoebe:

Till faint through irkesome wearinesse, adowne
Vpon the grassie ground her selfe she layd
To sleepe, the whiles a gentle slombring swowne
Vpon her fell all naked bare displayd;
The sunne-beames bright vpon her body playd,
Being through former bathing mollifide,
And pierst into her wombe, where they embayd
With so sweet sence and secret power vnspide,
That in her pregnant flesh they shortly fructifide.

Miraculous may seeme to him, that reades
So straunge ensample of conception;
But reason teacheth that the fruitfull seades
Of all things liuing, through impression
Of the sunbeames in moyst complexion,

Doe life conceiue and quickned are by kynd:
So after Nilus invndation,
Infinite shapes of creatures men do fynd,
Informed in the mud, on which the Sunne hath shynd.

Great father he of generation
is rightly cald, th'author of life and light;
And his faire sister for creation
Ministreth matter fit, which tempred right
With heate and humour, breedes the liuing wight.
So sprong these twinnes in wombe of Chrysogone,
Yet wist she nought thereof, but sore affright,
Wondred to see her belly so vpblone,
Which still increast, till she her terme had full outgone.

Appendix 3E

Philippson on Hesiod:

daβ der erste Ahnherr in allen Nachfahren forlebt. Das
ursprüngliche Sein, das dem Ahnherrn innewohnt, ist an sich
zeitlos; es erlischt nicht mit dem Tode des Ahnherrn, son-
dern stellt sich in seinen Nachkommen in zeitlicher Abfolge,
in immer erneuten Modifkationen dar.

Die Form, in der das Genos zur Darstellung kommt, ist
die Genealogie. . . . so dürfen wir aus dieser Offenbarung in
der Form der Genealogie schließen, daβ sich der Kosmos
als ein einmaliges, einheitliches, zeitloses Sein in vielfachen
Modifikationen entfaltet, denen dieses zeitlose Sein
immanent ist:

Die gesamten Erscheinungen, Kräfte und Gesetze des
Kosmos bilden eine genosartige Einheit.

Appendix 3F

Chaos in Ovid:

The reader interested in the differentiation of Chaos may
wish to see Ovid *Metamorphoses* 1.5-75, "unus erat toto
naturae vultus in orbe, quen dixere chaos," and *Ars Ama-
toria,* 2.467-68, "Prima fuit rerum confusa sine ordine moles,
/ Unaque erat facies sidera, terra, fretum," and Lucretius, *De
Rerum Natura,* 5, 434-439, "nec mare nec caelum nec magni
sidera mundi / nec similis nostris rebus res ulla videri, / sed

nova tempestas quaedam molesque coorta / omnigenis e principiis, discordia quorum / intervalla vias conexus pondera plagas / concursus motus turbabat proelia miscens," although they involve no kinship metaphor.)

Appendix 3G

Chaos in Milton:

> Before thir eyes in sudden view appear
> The secrets of the hoary deep, a dark
> Illimitable Ocean without bound,
> Without dimension, where length, breadth, and highth,
> And time and place are lost; where eldest Night
> And Chaos, Ancestors of Nature, hold
> Eternal Anarchy, amidst the noise
> Of endless wars, and by confusion stand.
> For hot, cold, moist, and dry, four Champions fierce
> Strive here for Maistry. . . .
>   Chaos Umpire sits,
> and by decision more imbroils the fray
> By which he Reigns: next him high Arbiter
> Chance governs all. Into this wild Abyss
> The Womb of nature and perhaps her Grave,
> Of neither Sea, nor Shore, nor Air, nor Fire,
> But all these in thir pregnant causes mixt
> Confus'dly, and which thus must ever fight,
> Unless th'Almighty Maker them ordain
> His dark materials to create more Worlds. . . .

Appendix 3H

Chaos in Spenser:

> For in the wide wombe of the world there lyes,
> In hatefull darkenesse and in deepe horrore,
> An huge eternall Chaos, which supplyes
> The substances of natures fruitfull progenyes.
>
> All things from thence doe their first being fetch,
> Which when as forme and feature it does ketch,
> Becomes a bodie, and doth then inuade
> The state of life, out of the griesly shade.
> That substance is eterne, and bideth so,

Ne when the life decayse, and forme does fade,
doth it consume, and into nothing go,
But chaunged is, and often altred to and fro.

Appendix 3I

Nothingness in Gower:

John the apostle evangelist in the gospel he wrote bears witness that in the beginning God created and made everything, but nothingness was made without him, so he says: Of which Saint Gregory, who afterwards expounded it, wisely, through divine inspiration, apprised us of the form of nothingness, saying that nothingness contains in itself only the name of sin, for sin annihilates all good. First when God made the heavens, of all spiritual angels, one Lucifer was principal; but of that sin that was mortal he fell from the heavens through nothingness towards hell; Sin was the source of all evils, turning joys into sorrows, from high to low changing the ranks (places). Nothingness is sin the disloyal, because by its will and its counsels it wishes to annihilate whatever God made.

Jehan l'apostre evangelist / En l'evangile qu'il escrist / Tesmoigne q'au commencement / Dieux creat toute chose et fist, / Mais nient fuist fait sanz luy, ce dist; / Dont saint Gregoire sagement, / Qui puis en fist l'exponement, / Par le divin inspirement / Du nient la forme nous aprist, / Disant que nient en soy comprent / Le noun du pecché soulement, / Car pecché tous biens anientist. / Primer quant dieus ot fait les cieux, / Des tous angres espiritieux / Un Lucifer fuist principals; / Mais du pecché q'estoit mortieux / Chaoit de les celestieux / Au nient devers les infernalx: / Pecché fuist source de les mals, / Tornant les joyes en travals, / De halt en bas changeant les lieux: / Nient est pecché ly desloyals, / Car par son vuill et ses consals / Volt anientir quanque fist dieux. (ll. 49-72)

4 *Causation*

4.1 Introduction to the rest of this book

Until now, I have been investigating connections between cognition, language, and literature by analyzing specific metaphors phrased in the language of kinship terms. Hereafter, I look more generally at our *conceptual* apparatus and the role our concept of genealogy plays in it.

4.2 A problem with causation

Here are some examples of a certain type of causal statement:

Night produces fear.
Despair causes madness.
Age causes sickness.
Filth causes stench and disease.
Fear results in superstition.
Solitude causes anxiety.
Necessity leads to invention.
Violence springs from fear.
Idleness causes vice.
Toil results in fame.
Hatred derives from misunderstanding.
Gambling is a consequence of avarice.
Anger causes violence.
Suicide comes from despair.

Idleness causes theft.
Fog causes disaster.

There is a problem with these and related causal statements. What notion of causation do we use to understand these sentences? Is there just one?

4.3 Some failures to solve the problem

There are some well-known characterizations of ways we conceive of causation. Each of them has been shown to account for how we understand some particular kind of causal phenomena. Can any of these well-known characterizations account for the type of causation we see expressed in these examples? I will survey them to show that none can. This will not mean that these characterizations are wrong or that they should be replaced, but rather that they are not adequate to account for the particular kind of causal statement under consideration. This will naturally lead us to the question, Is there yet some different conception of causation that accounts for these causal statements?

Causation as regularity

We may think of causation in terms of invariant sequences. Whenever an effect is invariantly conjoined actually with certain conditions, we may think of those conditions as its cause.

Causation as regularity cannot account for the type of causal statement under consideration because none of the causal statements implies an invariant sequence. We do not understand "Night causes fear" to mean that whenever nightfall comes around, everybody starts quaking. We do not understand "Despair causes madness" to mean that madness always follows hard upon despair.

Causation as necessary and sufficient conditions

We can think of the cause of an effect as all the conditions necessary for that effect to happen. The set of all the conditions necessary for a particular effect constitutes a condition sufficient to cause the effect. So we can think of the cause of an effect as a set of necessary and sufficient conditions.

Causation as necessary and sufficient conditions cannot account for how we understand the causal statements under consideration. A statement like "Night produces fear" is a causal generalization. We may use such this generalization to account for a specific case in which we feel that a specific night was very important in bringing about a specific case of fear, but we do not feel that, in general, fear can never arise in the absence of night, or that, in general, fear must result whenever it is night. In other words, we do not feel that, in general, night is either a necessary or a sufficient condition for fear. So we cannot account for this causal generalization as a case of *causation as necessary and sufficient conditions*. Similarly, despair is not a necessary or sufficient condition for madness, and toil is not a necessary or sufficient condition for fame.

In no case do we even understand the mentioned cause as standing for some determinate causal complex of conditions we could express. Despair must interact with many other things to produce madness, and we do not have a sense that we can list in unique or determinate or discrete or even finite fashion the other conditions involved in the interaction. We do not need to be able to list them in order to understand that causation is involved. We do not need even to think that in principle they could be listed.

Causation as action (direct manipulation, applied force)

We can think of causation as someone directly manipulating some preexisting objects from one state into another state. More generally, we can think of an application of force that transforms one state into another as a cause. More generally still, we can think of any action transforming one state into another as a cause. *Causation as action* requires an initial state, a transformation, and a consequent final state. *Causation as direct manipulation* further requires a source material distinct from the causer.

Causation as direct manipulation, applied force, or *action* cannot account for the causal statements under consideration, because in them there need be no source material and no transformation. "Idleness causes vice" implies no causative action. "Necessity causes invention" is not understood, even metaphorically, as necessity manipulating something into being invention, the way we whittle a piece of wood into a cane. Rather, first there was nothing, and then there was the invention.

Causation as reason

We can think of a ratiocinative agent having an intentional reason for doing something. This kind of reason can be thought of as a kind of cause. If we think of a parent striking a child because the child disobeyed, we say the parent had a *reason*. This is different from thinking of a parent striking a child because the parent is drunk. Being drunk does not constitute an intentional reason for the violence but rather a cause.

Causation as reason cannot account for the type of causal statement under consideration because none of the causes can be thought of as an intentional reason for an act. Age is not an intentional reason, or purpose, for sickness.

Causation as interpersonal motivation

Sometimes one agent gives another agent a motive for a voluntary act, as in "John bribed Thomas to feign illness." We can think of the motivating agent (John) as the cause ("John got Tom to feign illness"). *Causation as interpersonal motivation* cannot account for the causal statements we are considering, because the effects in these cases need not be voluntary, no motive need be involved, and the cause need not be seen as an agent operating on something, including another agent. "Age causes sickness" does not mean that sickness is voluntary, or that the sick thing knows of some motive for its being sick, or that age operated on some preexisting thing, including an agent, to bring about sickness. "Fog causes disaster" does not mean that fog gives anything a motive.

I conclude that none of the well-known ways we conceive of causation accounts for the type of causal statement under consideration.

4.4 Causation as progeneration

Let us put aside this problem for a moment and return to the familiar ground of kinship metaphor. We will ultimately be helped in our analysis by doing so. In chapter 2, I introduced the metaphoric inference pattern *causation as progeneration*. I also introduced the metaphoric inference pattern *lineage*, which accounts for the principal use of kinship metaphor, namely, to express paths by which things in the world, the mind, and behavior can spring from one another. And I explained that *lineage* is a special case of *causation as progeneration*, except when it is a special case of *similarity*.

Let us look at some of the examples from chapter 2:

Sickenesses, or their true mother, Age
Stench, diseases, and old filth, their mother
Sable Night, mother of dread and fear
The moon is the mother of pathos and pity.
Solitude is the mother of anxieties.
The true child of vanity is violence.
Babylon is the mother of harlots and abominations.
George Washington is the father of his country.

The conceptual metaphor we need to understand these statements is, as I discussed in chapter 2, CAUSATION IS PRO-GENERATION. What is the conceptual mapping between causation and progeneration? What components of progeneration are involved in the mapping? What conception of causation results from the mapping?

Personification

In the mapping CAUSATION IS PROGENERATION, cause corresponds to parent (mother, father), and effect corresponds to child (son, daughter). Mother, father, parent, son, daughter, and child are persons. *Causation as progeneration* preserves some aspects of *person* in the mapping. For a sequence to be understood as progenerative causation, the cause and effect must be able to be personified, in some minimal ways, as follows:

Cohesion and individuation. A person is an individual, a cohesive unit. A cause or effect expressed through kinship metaphor must be an individuated, cohesive conceptual unit.

If asked what *night* is, or *age*, or *sickness*, or *fog*, we feel that we know, that we have an answer, and that these concepts have an individuated cohesion. We do not feel that our conception of *night* is so vague, unmanageable, or illimitable that we cannot answer the question. There are other things—like the myriad, borderless processes and material of biology somehow involved in progeneration—that do not have this stamp of conceptual individuation and cohesion. Separate individuated effects of a cause cannot be one child, but they may, since parents can have many children, be expressed as a set of children ("Babylon is the mother of harlots and abominations").

Duration. A person abides. The cause and effect expressed through the kinship metaphor must have some duration, conceptually or actually, that can be thought of as a life.

A general category (e.g., night, filth, age, disaster, fog) has these properties of conceptual cohesion, individuation, and duration. So do many states of the world (e.g., war), the mind (e.g., anger), and behavior (e.g., violence), including some negative states (e.g., purposelessness, idleness).

I think that this requirement of conceptual cohesion, individuation, and duration partially explains why we find certain kinds of words occurring as cause and effect in causal generalizations expressed through kinship metaphor. The reader may check his own intuition to see whether he agrees with my judgment that "despair" implies greater conceptual cohesion, individuation, and duration than does "despairing," and that "despairing" in turn implies greater conceptual cohesion, individuation, and duration than does "being desperate." We prefer to say "Suicide is the child of despair" instead of "Suicide is the child of despairing" or "Suicide is the child of being desperate." We feel comfortable, however, saying "Gambling is the child of avarice" or "Hatred is the child of misunderstanding" because we have only the gerundive nominals "gambling" and "misunderstanding" in the language, and no derived nominals (like "despair") that might replace them.

Nature of the causation

Generic versus specific causes and effects. A specific and localized instance of causation can be expressed using a specific parent and child. We may say, for instance, of the institution of the United States, that "George Washington was the father of his country." Since this expresses a specific instance of causation, the verb can situate it in the past. We can also say "that mother of mischief, the Stamp Act." This makes the cause a specific mother and refers to localized instances of causation. But such statements are not causal generalizations. An enduring causal generalization requires a generic cause and a generic effect and is situated in the enduring present. Generics can both have taken place in the past and have the potential for taking place in the future. A generic parent can both have been a parent in a specific birth in the past and have the potential for being the parent in future births. Consequently, where kinship metaphor is used to present a causal generalization, the cause and effect must be generic, and the verb must be the enduring present, as in "Solitude is the mother of anxieties."

Efficacy. A mother is known to have produced a certain child, is thought to have had a special latent efficacy (capacity, power) to produce it, and is usually perceived as retaining this same efficacy. The mother and the child are connected in our idealized cognitive models of kinship as efficacy and result. A father is known to have been uniquely instrumental to the conception of a thing and is thought to have had a special latent power for initiating—and sometimes parenting—the thing.

Consequently, in causal generalizations expressed through *causation as progeneration,* if the cause is a mother, then the cause is known to have produced a certain effect, is thought to have had a special efficacy to produce it, and is usually perceived as retaining this same efficacy. The cause has a special efficacy to produce the effect, even if it never does again. If the cause is a father, then the cause is uniquely instrumental to the conception of the thing and had a special latent efficacy for initiating it.

Nonisolation of cause. I have said that the cause in cases of *causation as progeneration* must have conceptual individuation, cohesion, and duration. But conceptual unity does not mean causal isolation. When *causation as progeneration* presents a conceptually individuated, cohesive, and enduring unit as a cause, it does not thereby isolate out the causal conditions. *Mother* has high conceptual individuation, cohesion, and duration. But a mother is not the only thing involved in producing a child. Conceptually very distinct, a mother is nonetheless not the exact sum total of the causal conditions. Mother and father must interact with each other, and with a great deal else, to produce a child. To point out a mother does not deny that a father exists, does not imply that the mother *in vacuo* logically or necessarily or actually entailed the child, or that conditions could not prevent the mother from producing a similar child again. As a *concept*, a mother is isolable from her world. As a *cause*, she is not isolable from the rest of her world, which contributes to the causation. We do not feel that we could hope to separate out exactly the conditions, the parts of conception, gestation, and nurturing, that led to the existence of a child as he is.

Consequently, in cases of *causation as progeneration*, referring to one cause does not deny that other causes exist, or imply that the cause *in vacuo* logically or necessarily or actually entailed the effect, or that conditions could not prevent the mentioned cause from producing a similar effect again. The cause is not isolated or isolable from its world. We do not need to have the sense that we could separate out exactly the necessary and sufficient conditions that led to the effect, or even that in principle such a list of isolable conditions exists.

Nondeterminism. We are certain that a mother produced her specific child in the past. But such certainty about a specific instance of causation in the past must be distinguished from determinism in the causal generalization. A mother does not deterministically produce a child. We do not understand her existence and properties as entailing the existence and properties of the child she in fact happened to give birth to. She must have had some child to be a mother, but we can understand that she might not have had that specific child. Her existence in the present does not deterministically produce another child identical to the last. The same mother might give birth to several children who differ in character and appearance. Consequently, in cases of *causation as progeneration*, we understand that the cause does not deterministically entail the effect and that the same cause can have different effects, even under similar conditions. Mothers are not deterministic as generalized causes.

Regularity and sufficiency unnecessary. A mother need not regularly produce children even though she may appear to be in the same circumstances as those in which she had earlier produced children. Consequently, in cases of *causation as progeneration*, the cause need not regularly produce the effect. This also explains that the cause need not be sufficient to produce the effect.

Necessity unnecessary. Many different mothers might have similar children. Consequently, in cases of *causation as progeneration*, the cause need not be necessary to produce the effect. Other causes can produce the same effect.

Something from nothing. A child appears out of nowhere—not exactly nowhere, but out of things or components that are in themselves relatively insignificant or imperceptible (e.g., sperm and egg). Consequently, in cases of *causation as progeneration*, the creation must be of something of one order of significance out of things of an order of much lower significance.

Quickness. Birth is relatively quick. Gestation and nurturing are extended and gradual processes, but the actual coming into existence is quick. Perhaps more accurately, our perception of the individuation of the child is quick. First, the fetus is contained in the mother. The mother is the whole, and the fetus is part of the whole. To say of this situation that the whole is the mother of the part is simply to describe the facts of the source domain of progeneration. Then, at the moment of birth, the part acquires an individuation distinct from the whole. We still feel that *mother and child* constitute a kind of conceptual unit by virtue of the progenerative bond, but they are not a conceptual unit like *pregnant woman* because the part has acquired a high individuation of its own. Consequently, in cases of *causation as progeneration*, the effect may be gestated gradually and slowly (as in a thought that is gestated), or an effect may be nurtured gradually and slowly (as in a brainchild that is nurtured into a full-blown theory), but if the kinship metaphor focuses on the span of time during which the effect achieves individuation or we come to perceive the individuation, then that span of time must be discrete, discontinuous, and fast.

There are thus causal situations we cannot express in terms of kinship metaphor because they do not meet the characteristics that derive from the mapping CAUSATION IS PROGENERATION. We cannot say "Death is the child of decapitation" because, though the cause and effect can be personified in the minimal sense above, we conceive of decapitation as a deterministic sufficient condition for death. A phrase like "Your pushing me was the mother of my falling down" fails on several counts.

4.5 Causation as progeneration solves the problem

The point is now apparent that the characteristics of the conceptual metaphor CAUSATION IS PROGENERATION, which underlies our understanding of kinship metaphors expressing causation, match the characteristics of the unaccounted-for type of causal statement. Consequently, we can express each of those causal statements as a kinship metaphor:

Night produces fear.
Night is the mother of fear.

Despair causes madness.
Despair is the mother of madness.

Age causes sickness.
Age is the mother of sickness.

Filth causes stench and disease.
Filth is the mother of stench and disease.

Fear results in superstition.
Fear is the mother of superstition.

Solitude causes anxiety.
Solitude is the mother of anxiety.

Necessity leads to invention.
Necessity is the mother of invention.

Violence springs from fear.
Violence is the child of fear.

Idleness causes vice.

Idleness is the mother of vice.

Toil results in fame.
Toil is the father of fame.

Hatred derives from misunderstanding.
Hatred is the child of misunderstanding.

Ignorance causes suspicion.
Ignorance is the mother of suspicion.

Gambling is a consequence of avarice.
Gambling is the child of avarice.

Anger causes violence.
Violence is the child of anger.

Suicide comes from despair.
Suicide is the child of despair.

Idleness causes theft.
Idleness is the mother of theft.

Fog causes disaster.
Fog is the mother of disaster.

I have shown that there are causal statements that cannot be accounted for by any of the usual explanations of how we conceive of causation. I have shown that we have the conceptual metaphor CAUSATION IS PROGENERATION. I have shown that the characteristics of CAUSATION IS PROGENERA-TION match the characteristics of the causal statements that are otherwise unaccounted for. It is natural to conclude therefore that we understand these otherwise unaccounted-for causal statements by virtue of the conceptual metaphor CAUSATION IS PROGENERATION.

But I cannot say that I have absolutely proved this conclusion. Such absolute proof is not possible, for the following reason. In theory, someone could come up with yet a different way we understand causation. He might demonstrate, as I have for CAUSATION IS PROGENERATION, that we possess this way of understanding causation, that this new way has the characteristics of CAUSATION IS PROGEN-ERATION needed to understand the unaccounted-for type of causal statement, and therefore that my hypothesis has a rival. I can only say that this scenario seems unlikely to me.

There is a different approach one might take to explaining my observations. I will call it the "abstractionist" approach. I want now to show that this approach must grant my main point, but nevertheless will still be wrong. An abstractionist explanation would run along these lines: "At the linguistic level of words, we may express causation by using words about progeneration. But this does not mean that at the conceptual level we ever understand causation in terms of progeneration. On the contrary, what is happening at the conceptual level is that we understand causation and progeneration independently of each other. We can notice similarities in them. We can combine these similarities into an abstraction that covers both cases. Then we can use words about one of the concepts to express the abstraction that also covers the other concept. But no conceptual metaphor is involved. Specifically, progeneration has the characteristic of something from nothing, and so does a kind of causation. This similar feature has been abstracted from the two domains into a notion of creation of something out of nothing. Whenever this similarity obtains, we can express causation in terms of progeneration."

This is wrong, because there are many causal events of something from nothing that cannot be expressed in terms of progeneration. A spontaneous, spectacular nose bleed, for example, seems like something from nothing, but we cannot say "Mary's spontaneous, spectacular nose bleed last night was the child of her not having strong nose veins."

The abstractionist might answer any such counterexample by adding to the abstraction those features needed to exclude the counterexample. He might say, "We have an abstract notion of something from nothing where the creative entity and the created entity have conceptual cohesion, individuation, and duration." But then there would be another class of counterexamples. For example, death can be something from nothing: "First everything was normal, and then he dropped dead." Cyanide and death have conceptual individuation, cohesion, and duration. And we can say "Cyanide causes death." But we cannot say naturally "Death is the child of cyanide" because we think of ingesting cyanide as a deterministic sufficient condition for death.

Finally, suppose the abstractionist includes all the features of CAUSATION IS PROGENERATION in his abstraction, so there will be no more counterexamples. He will then be saying that we have a concept of creation that has all the characteristics of CAUSATION IS PROGENERATION but is different from CAUSATION IS PROGENERATION, and that we use this concept to understand the problematic causal statements under consideration. He will then be granting the main point of this chapter so far.

But this account will still be wrong. If this concept of creation proposed were an abstraction from the two conceptual domains of causation and progeneration, then the connection between causation and progeneration via this abstraction should be symmetric. That is, we should be able to express progeneration in terms of causation, just as we express causation in terms of progeneration. But the connection is in fact strongly asymmetric. We can say "Solitude is the cause of anxiety" as "Solitude is the mother of anxiety," but we cannot say "Penelope is the mother of Telemachus" as "Penelope is the cause of Telemachus."

4.6 Relations among conceptions of causation

What are the relations between these various human conceptions of causation? How do they compare with scientific theories of causation?

Here I will say nothing normative or prescriptive about scientific theories of causation. I will not argue about their usefulness or propose changes in them. But often, as in Kant and Mill, someone argues that we have a single commonsense conception of causation and that this conception can be explained in terms of a scientific theory of causation. I will argue that such arguments are misguided. I think that the concept of efficacy (potential, power) in a cause is fundamental to certain kinds of human understanding of causation and cannot accurately be reduced to concepts of action, manipulation, will, or necessary and sufficient antecedent conditions. So I am responding here to a long tradition of theorizing about human conceptions of causation.*

*In particular, there is a robust tradition of citing the testimony of

I need to sketch for starters some main issues in the philosophy of causation. Theoretical natural sciences, at least before the twentieth century, sought to resolve a given system of interest into elements, and to define relations on the elements such that knowledge of those elements and those relations allowed one to predict the system. Thus in Newtonian point mechanics, only the constant mass and the variables position and velocity are important, and relations called laws are defined upon them. Knowing the constant mass, the values of the variables at a fixed time, and the laws, we can predict both the past and the future of the system.

Concern over the status of these laws and other causal statements prompted Hume's analysis of causation (*Inquiry*, 1741, secs. 4-7). I will characterize Hume's analysis as a regularity theory: it claims that causal statements are short-hand for regularly observed sequences, that causes and effects are merely changes constantly conjoined. It rejects necessary connection between cause and effect. The classic accompanying paradigmatic illustration is the collision of two billiard balls: we never see a connection, merely one occurrence and then another. As Mill (*System of Logic*, 1843, vol. 1, chap. 5, sec. 3) and Searle ("Causation," 1983) discuss, this

---

language to clarify the concept of causation. The past four decades have seen analyses of causation based on ancillary analyses of conditionals (see Downing 1958, Mackie 1975, O'Connor 1951, Schneider 1952, Sosa 1975, Stalnaker and Thomason 1970, and von Wright 1957), counterfactuals (see Bennet 1974, Chisholm 1946, Finch 1957, Lewis 1973, Mackie 1962, Popper 1949, Schock 1961, and Sellars 1958), tense, time, and temporal priority of cause over effect (see Ayer 1956, Black 1956, Dummett 1954, and Pears 1956), and subjunctivity, modality, and possible world semantics (see Bennett 1974, Downing 1958, Lewis 1973, Schneider 1952, Schock 1961, Sellars 1958, Stalnaker and Thomason 1970, and von Wright 1957). Hart and Honoré (1959), in their authoritative *Causation in the Law*, argue that philosophical theories of causation are false to human concepts of responsibility, blame, tort, harm, risk, negligence, and crime; they appeal for evidence to the representation of causation in language and the translation of that representation into statutory and common law. Lakoff and Johnson (1980), in "Causation: Partly Emergent and Partly Metaphorical," cite metaphor systems to show that causation is based on a prototype of direct manipulation. Researchers in natural language processing, considering what talents a processor needs for representation of causality, have also turned to language. See Wilks (1977) for a survey.

theory and illustration fail to correspond with human intuitions of causation.

The observations that there are real invariant sequences (such as day following night) where we do not infer causation and that, of the many conditions obtaining before an event, only some—the *conditiones sine quibus non*—are considered pertinent to causation, have led to the question: Which conditions regularly conjoined with an effect are in fact necessary—logically or actually—for the event to occur? It has been proposed, with many small variations, that the cause of something is all the conditions constantly conjoined with it such that each was actually—not logically—necessary for the event. It has also been argued that if one adopts the principle of uniformity—that like causes have like effects—then the set of conditions necessary for an effect will be sufficient to produce it again. Cause is then a set of necessary and sufficient conditions. Obvious difficulties then arise in considering cases where the same cause seems to have different effects, where the same effect can have different causes, and where one effect seems in fact to have more than one sufficient cause preceding it. Further, if causes are necessary and sufficient conditions, it can be claimed that there is no sharp distinction between cause and effect, a position taken by both Bertrand Russell (1917) and J. M. E. McTaggart (1934). (See Chisholm and Taylor 1960.)

There is a different, recent, smaller tradition that claims philosophy has been overly influenced in its discussions of causation by the use of the term in theoretical natural science and that this scientific sense of causation is in fact a metaphorical extension of historically earlier, experiential senses. R. G. Collingwood (1940, pp. 285-327) claims and supports philologically that, in its historically earliest sense, a cause is whatever gives a motive for performing a free and deliberate act; whatever gives the motive *causes* the act. Collingwood explains that this sense of "cause" can be translated as "induce," "persuade," "urge," "force," "compel," and so on.

Collingwood claims that a second sense developed historically out of the root sense of *causation as interpersonal motivation*. This second sense is that used in practical sciences of nature, where the effect is an event in nature, and

its cause is an event or state of things such that if we produce or prevent the event or state we thereby produce or
prevent the effect (e.g., turning a switch causes a light to go
on; unplugging a lamp prevents a light from going on). The
third sense, allegedly derived from the second, is the sense
used in theoretical natural science, which Collingwood
claims is internally conflicted because the components of its
definition are mutually incompatible.

Collingwood's second sense of cause I will characterize as
causation as action. For Collingwood, *causation as action*
derives from *causation as interpersonal motivation*. Other
Action theorists include Douglas Gasking (1955), Georg
Henrik von Wright (1971), George Lakoff and Mark Johnson (1980), G. E. M. Anscombe (1971, pp. 8-9), and R. F.
Holland (as quoted in Mackie [1974, p. 133]). Lakoff and
Johnson view the various senses of causation as metaphorical
extensions of direct bodily manipulation by people. Gasking
argues that our sense of causation is grounded in manipulation: when we have a general manipulative technique which
results in a certain sort of event *A*, we speak of producing *A*
by this technique. For all these Action theorists, *causation as
direct manipulation* is the core of *causation as action*.

What are the relationships between these various conceptions of causation and *causation as progeneration*? I will
compare them on the basis of what each has to say about isolation of causal conditions, efficacy, prediction and explanation, motive and reason, action, and kinds of things that can
be causes and effects.

Isolation of causal conditions

Causation as regularity, as *necessary and sufficient conditions*, and as *action* are very close conceptually in all assuming that we can separate those occurrences involved in the
causation from those that are not. An occurrence is either
indispensably part of the causation or it has nothing to do
with the causation. For a regularly occurring event, the conditions isolated out are the same under all three conceptions.

Causation as progeneration conflicts strongly with these
other conceptions of causation on this point. Under *causation as progeneration*, causes are not *isolated* from their

worlds: a cause is never seen as a set of necessary or sufficient conditions that can be set apart from the world in which they participate. A cause rather is a salient power. To say that night is the mother of annoyance or the mother of sleep does not mean that night, by itself, causes annoyance or sleep. Other conditions are important, too. There is no notion in *causation as progeneration* that precisely the list of all the necessary conditions could ever be sorted out. The model implicit in kinship metaphor is not reductive. It illuminates salient conditions and marks them as having had the power to produce. This nonreduction derives from the nature of progeneration: we cannot hope to separate out exactly the conditions, the parts of conception, gestation, and nurturing, that led to the existence and nature of a given child as he or she is. Mill, critiquing Hume, noted that we seldom see a single antecedent followed by a single consequence. *Causation as progeneration* shows a sensitivity even greater than Mill's to cause as the whole of the situation from which an effect springs. There is no attempt to isolate which conditions are necessary and which sufficient but rather a view that the conditions interact to produce the effect. The conditions are viewed not as a sum but as an organic whole. Which of these conditions could be absent without changing the effect is not considered an important question. Locating parts of the causal complex by asking counterfactual questions* is altogether peripheral to the concept of causation behind kinship metaphor. For example, the many complicated debates in sciences of the human over whether *nature* or *nurture* causes a certain phenomenon, over whether a phenomenon is to be traced back to what is *innate* or what is *acquired*, cannot be phrased as such under *causation as progeneration*. Parents, *salient* causes, cannot be isolated from environments. Some causes are more salient than others, but they are not isolable or complete. Parent and environment are indissolubly interactive.

Under *causation as progeneration* the whole of the condi-

---

*That is, for a given effect y, asking of every antecedent x, "If x had not been the case, would y still have been the case?" and taking as cause the set of all and only such x for which the answer to the question is "no."

tions or environment can be the cause, as is shown by expressions like "Mother Earth," "Father Time," and all the earlier examples of *place and time as parent*. Consider:

the earth, great mother of us all

Aristotle sayth that the erthe is moder and the sonne fader of trees.

Time . . . Thou art the father of occasion dear.

Daughters of London, you which bee / Our golden mines, and furnish'd Treasurie

Babylon is the mother of harlots and abominations.

Jerusalem! . . . Mother of pity and dishonorable forgiveness

As a child of the modern era, I believe that there are all sorts of physical regularities.

Monday's child is fair of face,
Tuesday's child is full of grace.

Such examples present the entire environment as the cause. It makes as little sense to ask which of the conditions in the environment were necessary and sufficient as it does to ask what characteristics can be removed from the mother (or the mother's world) and still have her gestate and nurture the same child. The traditions of empiricism, analysis, and logical atomism and the philosophy of language descendant from them might be said, somewhat oversimply, to see reality as a linear sum of facts. But in *causation as progeneration*, the whole is more than the sum of its parts; reality is nonlinear; there are organic wholes with emergent properties. In the analytic tradition, it makes sense to analyze causation by breaking the whole into atoms and asking just what combination of atoms produces the effect. In *causation as progeneration*, this process of resolution and composition is seen as misguided and factitious. Salience is not separability, and highlighting a power as a cause does not mean reducing the whole to a subset of its components.

Efficacy in the cause to produce the effect

   Causation as progeneration is very far from both *Causation as necessary and sufficient conditions* and *causation as regular-*

ity on the issue of efficacy, but it is distinguished from each in different ways.

Causation as regularity absolutely excludes any connection between cause and effect other than invariant conjunction. In *causation as progeneration*, on the contrary, there must be a strong necessary connection of efficacy between the cause and the effect. (This conflict between *causation as regularity* and *causation as progeneration* might not have surprised Hume, who claimed merely that we have no logical justification for inferring necessary connection.)

Causation as necessary and sufficient conditions is virtually always discussed as if it too excludes the concept of efficacy. If *causation as necessary and sufficient conditions* is understood as including the notion of efficacy, then the efficacy must be *deterministic*, in the sense that if the necessary and sufficient conditions obtain, the effect must result. *Causation as progeneration* is nondeterministic.*

I have been referring to the "efficacy" of the cause and will continue to do so, but "power" or "potential" would also serve. Though many philosophers have endeavored to eradicate the concept of power or potential from concepts of causation, it is fundamental. Science, dismissing the concept of potential as an ultimate explanation and relying instead on antecedent sufficient and necessary conditions, has impressed us thoroughly, and rightly so, with its conquests. It has had a thing or two to say about certain kinds of human happenings, such as heart failure, genetics, and slips of the tongue. But it has failed to illuminate the nature of human voluntary happenings, which seem to require a fundamental concept of potential. This can be seen in statements such as "He can

---

*I have found two examples of kinship metaphor which might seem to suggest determinism in the world, but the determinism is of an altogether global, vague, abstract, unknowable, and unspecifiable sort, as if to argue that our notions of necessity are in fact nondeterministic. Neither expresses a deterministic chain of causation. These examples are "Necessity! thou mother of the world" and "Hope the best, but hold the Present fatal daughter of the Past." The first means that the world as a whole results from some sort of necessity, and the determinism, if it is implied, comes from the word "necessity" rather than from the kinship metaphor. The second suggests that somehow the present must follow from the past, but the determinism, if it is implied, comes from "fatal" rather than the kinship metaphor.

do it if he tries," which does not reduce to a case of enablement in the way "He can do it if he studies" does. Nor does "He can do it if he tries" reduce to will and action. Rather, it requires a meaning for "can" based on potential. "Can," historically, has taken the place of "may," which is linked with "might," which implies power, potency, potential: the Almighty is he who can do anything. The concept of potential here cannot be resolved away. The basic idea behind "can" is not action, or at least not only action, but also power, a different concept. Indeed, *the things you can do are the things you can leave undone.* This is not the case with natural causation as usually conceived: the acid can etch the metal but it cannot not etch the metal. So there is a crucial demarcation between *causation as necessary and sufficient conditions* and *causation as efficacy or potential.* Progeneration models the cause as possessing potential which it need not enact.

Because they exclude the concept of efficacy, *causation as regularity* and *as necessary and sufficient conditions* have great difficulty in explaining unique events or origins, but *cause as efficacy* has no difficulty at all. For the Pythagoreans, number—and indeed the universe—had a unique generation out of the unit (see Kirk and Raven 1957, p. 243). Throughout the *Theogony,* the *Enuma Elish,* and the Egyptian *Memphite Theology,* a unique component of reality can have a unique cause, a single creation.

In *causation as progeneration,* the efficacious mother must precede the child effect, but the absence of efficacy in *causation as necessary and sufficient conditions* has produced a confusion over whether an effect can precede its cause. (See Ayer 1956, Chisholm and Taylor 1960, Dray 1959, Dummett 1954, Dummett 1964, Gorovitz 1964, and Swinburne 1966.)

Causation as Action agrees with *causation as progeneration* in its presupposition that the cause has efficacy or power. In *causation as progeneration,* parents have power to progenerate. In *causation as action,* the agent has the power to perform the manipulation, or, more generally, something has the power to act.

Prediction and explanation

In *causation as progeneration*, causal statements are not seen as fast predictions or complete explanations. A mother need not have another child. She might not even have happened to have the first. But she is the preeminent feature in his progeneration, and we mark her as having had, and typically still having, a latent power to progenerate. In *causation as progeneration*, there is no handful of relations to be defined on a system that will empower us to make deterministic predictions. Sickness need not always accompany age for age to be the mother of sickness.

Causation as regularity and *causation as necessary and sufficient conditions* usually have their utility as tools of prediction and explanation. This is also usually the case for *causation as action* when the action is explained as a necessary or sufficient condition or as part of an invariant sequence. But sometimes, *causation as action* is used not to predict or explain but rather to assign responsibility. For example, leaving a can of gasoline next to a house already on fire may be neither a necessary condition for the house burning to the ground nor part of an invariant sequence, but it is part of a recipe of action potentially useful for assigning blame.

Motive and reason

A motive is a kind of reason, so *causation as interpersonal motivation* and *causation as reason* overlap, but *causation as interpersonal motivation* situates the cause in the motivating agent, and *causation as reason* situates it in the motive (reason).

In cases where events and states in the world, the mind, and behavior fit the characteristics of *causation as progeneration* and can also be seen as motives or reasons, there is an overlap between *causation as progeneration, causation as interpersonal motivation*, and *causation as reason*. We can say, for example, "Bribery is the mother of corruption."

I have found no kinship metaphor that cites a motivating person as a cause. I have found one kinship metaphor that mentions a motivating person but prefers to cite the psychological state as the cause: "If your Highness keep your purport, you will shock him even to death, or baser courses, children of despair." I have found another kinship metaphor that could be understood through either or both of *causation as progeneration* and *causation as interpersonal motivation*. It cites as cause something (the Stamp Act) that could be understood as metaphorical motivating agent or metaphorical parent or both: "I congratulate you on the repeal of that mother of mischief, the Stamp Act."

But aside from this overlap, *causation as progeneration* is far from *causation as interpersonal motivation* since in *causation as progeneration* the cause need be neither a motive nor a motivating agent. We can say "Night causes fear" and "Night is the mother of fear" but not "Night is the motive of fear" or "Night is the motivating agent of fear." Progeneration is not persuasion.

Collingwood claims that *causation as interpersonal motivation* is historically *the* basic sense of cause, but it can at most be historically *a* basic sense of cause.

Historically, as far back as I can trace in Western literature, *causation as progeneration* has been very natural and frequent. Indeed, many myths of creation and other prephilosophic cosmogonies, which are often among the very earliest written records of any civilization, use *causation as progeneration* repeatedly in their exposition of the causation of the world. Certainly this is true of the Greek and ancient Near Eastern civilizations. So it cannot be maintained that there is in Western history a conception of causation prior to *causation as progeneration*, or, more generally, to *causation as efficacy*.

Action (applied force, direct manipulation)

Causation as regularity dispenses with the concept of action. *Causation as necessary and sufficient conditions* analyzes apparent action into other terms.

Causation as progeneration requires no agent who is an actor, no act, no substance to be acted on, and no active transformation. It will, however, permit some actions (e.g., toil) to be causes, because actions not only manipulate states but also progenerate consequences. And, unlike Causation as Action, *causation as progeneration* will allow an action (e.g., suicide) to be an effect, since mind can lead to behavior under *lineage*.

Causation as progeneration and *causation as action* both

require efficacy when they account for an initial physical entity becoming a final physical entity, but *causation as action* places the efficacy in the external manipulator of the initial physical entity, and *causation as progeneration* places it in the initial physical entity itself. (Contrast "John built a desk" with "The acorn is the father of the oak" or "The child is the father of the man.") But it seems to me that there are cases where the efficacy might be understood as both internal and external to the substance, as in "Water . . . was by some thought to be the Mother of Earth." Water has a kind of efficacy to produce earth, as in the Egyptian creation myth where earth emerges from the water. But the sun may also be thought of as acting upon the water by evaporating it to allow the earth to emerge.

I have found not a single kinship metaphor involving bodily manipulation, and very few that even vaguely suggest that the action of a human being causes a physical event. Consider "George Washington was the father of his country." Such an example suggests that not just human action but also human vision, ideas, character, and judgment form the cause; and the result is not a physical event but an amorphous state.

Causation as progeneration and *causation as action* conflict strongly when static conditions and negative conditions and omissions are viewed as causes, as in "Night is the mother of Sloth" and "Purposelessness is the mother of crime," or in more standard statements such as that the fog caused the plane crash, lack of fuel caused the plane crash, or failure to radio the tower caused the plane crash. In these cases, it is hard to see action as involved. The efficacy resides in the condition (fogginess, lack of fuel, failure to communicate) and not anything outside it.

Often Action theorists take it as obvious that *causation as direct manipulation* is, as Piaget suggests, the child's earliest sense of cause. I do not see any reason for assuming this to be true. The power of the sun to heat us, of the wind to chill us, of others (especially parents) to touch or hurt us, of the empty stomach to make us unhappy—in general, of something to produce something—must be felt very early. It makes evolutionary sense that, before a child can manipulate (or persuade or be persuaded), he should be able to notice what in the world has the power to produce what. What can make him warm? What can make a loud noise? What can produce milk? What can make him cold? It seems to me unlikely that a child's knowledge of manipulative recipes would be developmentally prior to his knowledge that certain things have power to produce certain effects.

In terms of the historical literary data, neither *causation as progeneration* nor *causation as direct manipulation* can be reduced to the other, and it seems to me that this is the case conceptually as well, even though they both require efficacy. Myths of creation use both, as when Ouranos and Gaia beget Kronos, Kronos castrates Ouranos, and the fluids· of the rejected member impregnate the earth.

Kinds of things that can be causes and effects

Causation as necessary and sufficient conditions will permit any conditions—and *causation as regularity* any regularly occurring conditions—to be thought of as either cause or effect. Therefore, *causation as necessary and sufficient conditions* allows one to embrace easily the principle of uniformity, namely, that for any condition or any change, there must be a cause. Although it makes evolutionary sense that seeking causal models for everything would improve fitness, I can see no compelling reason to embrace the principle of uniformity as an a priori belief about reality.

The other conceptions of causation restrict the types of cause and effect they will account for. *Causation as action* requires a cause that can be conceived of, at least metaphorically, as an action, and an effect that can be conceived of, at least metaphorically, as the transformation of an initial state into a final state. *Causation as interpersonal motivation* requires one cause that can be conceived of, at least metaphorically, as a motivating agent, and another cause that can be conceived of, at least metaphorically, as the voluntary act of the motivating agent. *Causation as reason* requires a cause that can be conceived of, at least metaphorically, as a reason some ratiocinative entity might have, and an effect that can be conceived of, at least metaphorically, as the mental or physical behavior of this ratiocinative entity resulting from that reason.

Causation as progeneration requires causes and effects that can be personified, in the sense that they must be conceptually or actually cohesive, individuated, and enduring. The cause must be efficacious, nondeterministic, and nonisolated. The effect must be something from nothing* and quickly born.

Let us look for a moment at a few characteristics of the effect—quickly born, highly individuated, and something from nothing—to see how thoroughly *causation as progeneration* differs from other conceptions of causation.

Concepts of causation derived from the theoretical natural sciences, based on regularity or necessary and sufficient conditions, and elaborated by the philosophical tradition of Hume and Mill, do not principally concern the creation of something out of nothing, or, more accurately, the creation of a final state qualitatively different from the initial state. It is fair, I think, to point for evidence to the classic example of one billiard ball striking another: the final state is not qualitatively different from the initial state. First there is one billiard ball rolling toward a stationary billiard ball, and then there is one billiard ball rolling away from a (perhaps stationary) billiard ball. This is a mere alteration of circumstances, a rearranging of objects. Physical explanations of tides, chemical bonding, wave train interference, variables of pressure and volume and temperature of a gas, and orbits, for

---

*The belief that something could come from nothing appears to have at one time been more popular than some philosophers could bear. Parmenides writes, "Nor will the force of true belief allow that, beside what is, there could also arise anything from what is not" οὐδὲ ποτ' ἐκ μὴ ἐόντος ἐφήσει πίστιος ἰσχὺς γίνεσθαί τι παρ' αὐτό (Kirk and Raven 1957, p. 273).

In a key passage from the *De Rerum Natura* of Lucretius (1.149-73), which I place in the appendix to this chapter, we see a vehement rejection of the belief that something can come from nothing and an attempt to replace that belief with a progenerative explanation of creation and causation, a materialistic explanation of everything, including sensations and mental events. Lucretius maintains that, though many occurrences appear to arise from nothing, actually there is always a source material, and, very important, an efficacy in the source material to produce the result. This passage demonstrates how easy it is to identify "something from nothing" with progeneration. Lucretius argues that popular opinion has mistakenly identified them.

example, all have this common characteristic of change as an alteration or rearrangement of things without the production of something qualitatively different. Thus they do not cohere with *causation as progeneration*.

Cases exist in physics of the causation of something qualitatively of much higher significance than its source material: an earthquake, an eclipse, or an explosion, for example. These cases of causation could conceivably be understood by using *causation as progeneration*. But, tellingly, it is not such occurrences that theories of causation in the tradition of Hume select for focus or example. More tellingly, physics itself and science in general have long found themselves most competent at explaining phenomena where small differences in causes produce small differences in effects. As has been noted by mathematicians from Poincaré to Zeeman, physics is less adept at explaining cases where a small difference in causes produces great differences in effects, as, for instance, when very small differences in the treatment of a dog will cause it to attack: the attack is a sudden and qualitatively different thing from the preceding behavior.

Usually, science tries to explain such instances as the passing of an equilibrium point: a state of equilibrium will be upset by the smallest extra force. Consider, as an illustration, an inverted cone balanced on its tip. It tips over when the smallest force is applied at any point on the circumference of its base, because that upsets the equilibrium. But an equilibrium is just one point along a continuum of values, and the values on either side of equilibrium do not differ from it qualitatively. When an eclipse occurs, the positions of the two bodies are just values in a representation of space and time, and these values do not differ qualitatively from the values of the positions just before and after. An earthquake is the passing of an equilibrium point along continua of tectonic stress. My point is that although in these cases physics explains both the creation of something out of nothing and the occurrence of something (eclipse) quite unlike its source material, nonetheless the explanation represents the occurrence in terms of components not qualitatively different from the components of preceding or succeeding states. Paradigmatically, as with the billiard balls, it is all just continuous variation in the values of position and momentum.

This is not the kind of causation understood as progeneration.

Causation as action can also conflict with the creation of something from nothing. Direct manipulation usually concerns moving things around and rearranging environments. It usually concerns alteration rather than creation. To be sure, it sometimes concerns creation, as in the sculpting of marble. And in such cases, *causation as progeneration* can cohere with *causation as action*. But the gradual evolution of the sculpture evokes gestation rather than birth: a sculptor labors. The sharp palpability and definition of the marble as source material makes it less appropriate to conceive of the sculpting as birth and more appropriate to conceive of it as manipulation and gestation. Verbal art is much more aptly conceived of as birth: its quickness, and the sharp springing of highly individuated effects seemingly out of nowhere, fit *causation as progeneration* tightly.

Neither *causation as regularity* nor *causation as action* requires that the effect be a sharply completed. While a fetus is being gestated, we can think of the mother as making the baby, but when the baby is born, it is a sharply completed result: we cannot hand the baby back to her and ask her to gestate the eyes a little bit more, or work on the shoulder joints a bit. At the moment of birth, there is a conceptually individuated cause, and a conceptually individuated effect that is sharply complete as an effect. Differential equations, traditionally the prototype of predictive models in physics, do not require separate and individuated cause and effect. When we see or think of the propagation of electromagnetic waves, the motion of celestial bodies, the motion of gases, we can picture effect flowing into effect continuously and smoothly. At any arbitrary moment, we can call the state an effect, and the effect is not qualitatively different from states before or after. In physics, when an individuated effect happens, it is often resolved back into an explanation which diminishes the sense of individuation, as when a nuclear explosion is explained as a fission chain reaction in radioactive material of critical mass. And action can produce a rearrangement, alteration, or modification of objects that has no sharp distinction from an interim rearrangement, alteration, or modification. In munching on snacks, throwing things about, polishing or smoothing or moving things, there is rarely a sense of one effect highly individuated from interim effects and incapable of being carried further because of its completeness. We could munch a bit more, toss things a bit more, polish a little more. If someone is polishing a stone for us and hands it to us as finished, we can hand it back and ask for a bit more polishing. We have conventional end states for things like eating (i.e., when your plate is clean) and polishing (i.e., when we feel no rough spots), but we do not think of these as causal end states. *Causation as progeneration* requires a sharply completed effect that cannot be progenerated a bit further.

Causation as progeneration requires the effect to endure for a duration that can be conceived of as a life and to remain cohesive and complete during this lifespan. Although the effect may decay or diminish, it cannot fragment in the middle of its life into wholes perceived as distinct units. *Causation as regularity* and *causation as action* do not require this duration of completeness in the effect. Rake a pile of leaves together and watch them blow gradually away: *causation as direct manipulation* can capture that. Watch a cloud break up and grow diffuse, and the parts break again, and some parts rejoin, and so on: physics, meteorology, and action can handle that. *Causation as progeneration* cannot handle either one unless we either conceive of the effect as finished before the fragmentation or conceive of each fragmentation as a progeneration, making a series of progenerations.

To sum up: consider one paradigm of *causation as action*—someone moving objects around—and one paradigm of *causation as regularity*—the wind whirling wind cups about. In neither case must we see a sharply individuated effect. The effect need not be qualitatively different from its source material. The effect need not necessarily have a conceptual completeness that coheres during its life span, and the acquisition of sharp individuality, if it transpires at all, can be slow, continuous, nondiscrete. *Causation as progeneration* stands apart from these. It prototypically concerns individuated effects rapidly sprung (conceptually) out of nowhere, and enduring whole for a while.

Is causation one concept?

The various conceptions of causation involve different constituents, relations, functions, and transformations. It is not in the details of the conceptions that we will find some unifying similarity. There is no one feature (or set of features) common to each conception of causation that allows us to say that causation consists in having this feature (or set of features).

Nor are the various conceptions of causation united into one category by virtue of family resemblance. We say a set shows family resemblance when every two members significantly overlap, even though no feature is common to every member. It is not the case that every two conceptions of causation significantly overlap. *Causation as interpersonal motivation* and *causation as progeneration* have very little overlap. *Causation as progeneration* and *causation as necessary and sufficient conditions* also have very little overlap.

Nor is it the case that there is some one most basic experiential conception of causation from which we can metaphorically or metonymically derive all the others. There is a tendency throughout the extensive literature on causation to seek such an experiential basis of causation. To be sure, conceptions of causation have experiential bases such as direct manipulation by the human hand, the influence of the mind on behavior, the influence of the world on the mind, one physical event producing an immediately consequent physical event, birth, nurturing, and so on. But I do not see how one of these can serve as a basis for how we understand all the others.

What holds these conceptions together as varieties of the one concept, causation? They all have a similar cognitive *purpose* or *use*. Each conception gives us a way of understanding how some things can come to be. And each of these ways of understanding has proven helpful to us in dealing with our worlds. Each lets us group many different individual sequences of events under a given model of causation. This helps us represent such sequences conceptually, helps us access sequences related by a given model, and helps us understand new sequences in terms of known sequences and the models we use to understand them.

When we feel we have a model helpful for accounting for how something comes to be, we say we have located a cause. It is this similarity in what we do cognitively with these various conceptual models that allows us to group them together as varieties of what we thereby come to think of as one thing, *causation*.

This view conflicts with the opinions of all authors—including Collingwood, Gasking, von Wright, Lakoff and Johnson, even the extraordinarily insightful Hart and Honoré, and Thomas Reid, who will be discussed later—who try to root all causation in some one experiential model. I suspect, if I understand these authors correctly, that my view would be criticized on the ground that a concept must be rooted in an experience rather than an abstraction. But this does not seem to me to constitute a substantive objection. First, there is no disagreement that each of the varieties of causation is rooted in some experiential model. The debate is whether one of these experiential models can rightly be described as the basic stereotype from which the others derive. I do not see how that can be. But I would agree that there is no more fundamental human experience than having a model of a domain and using that model conceptually. To root causation in a sense of the similar use of models generally rather than in the specifics of any one model is to root it not in an academic abstraction but rather in the one preeminent human experience. Indeed, having a variety of models and using them cognitively is a far more universal and more practiced experience than having any one of the specific conceptions of causation and using it.

No doubt the reluctance to ground a unifying concept like causation in what appear to be abstractions rather than behaviors, in cognition rather than events, is partially a reaction to the tradition of Kant and the attempt to ground human cognition in abstractions like formal logic schemata and theoretical physics. Yet this grounding of causation in the use of conceptual models is a grounding in the most common cognitive experience rather than in an academic abstraction.

4.7 Progeneration and mind

There are conceptual realms where *causation as progenera-tion* has preeminence. The most conspicuous such realm is biology, but the most interesting is mind.

Sometimes we ruminate, gather mental wool, stare vacantly into space. Sometimes the unconscious churns diligently, without giving the conscious mind a clue. But, often, mental events—thoughts, ideas, feelings—are progenerations. They are not mere alterations of components or rearrangements of things but rather births of things of high significance. Though the cause may be conceptually individuated, cohesive, and enduring, just as a mother is, the mental event itself is a creation of something where there was nothing of equal status before, nothing that could be simply rearranged or altered to produce the state or event. On the one hand, the point at which the thought acquires its individuality is quick. Often it is as if an idea comes magically out of nothing. And language reflects this when it allows us to speak of an idea coming out of nowhere. On the other hand, the gestating and nurturing aspects of progeneration can aptly fit deliberative mental acts, while still allowing one to demarcate the moment of birth when the idea or concept or feeling becomes well-formed or is perceived as well-formed.

Theories of causation have largely ignored the mind, concerning themselves principally with physical events and, to a lesser extent, human actions. In some cases, science has attempted to elucidate the occurrence of mental acts by explaining them in terms of necessary and sufficient neurobiological conditions or predictable regularities, analogous to clockwork or computation. But we all sense that, regardless of the possible truth or falsity of this explanation, we do not usually conceive of mental events in these terms.

Action theories do not ignore mind entirely since they frequently talk about the desire of the agent to perform the action. Nonetheless, they focus on the action as the cause, and whatever it produces as the effect. This is true even of Thomas Reid (*Essays on the Active Powers of Man*, 1788, essay 4). Reid was one one of the earliest arguers against Hume and in favor of necessary connection between cause and effect. Reid pleads at length that causation is grounded in a sense of active power to produce a result, and he even mentions that effects can be "of thought, of will, or of motion." Nonetheless, because virtually his entire discussion concerns bodily action, he does not notice causation as progeneration or recognize the creation of something out of nothing. Indeed, for him a cause is a rearrangement or an alteration of things already extant. "The name of a *cause* and of an *agent,* is properly given to that being only, which, by its active power, produces some change in itself, or in some other being." This excludes birth, excludes the creation of a being, excludes creation of something out of nothing. Though Reid rightly noticed ways in which our conceptions of causation conflict with Hume's analysis ("All that is necessary to the production of any effect, is power in an efficient cause to produce the effect, and the exertion of that power," and "To prevent mistake, it is proper to observe, that a being may have a power at one time which it has not at another"), yet his focus on bodily action as active power prevents him from mentioning progeneration or, consequently, the progenerative aspect of mental events. Herein he typifies Action theorists, though he comes closest of all to considering mental events.

   H. L. A. Hart and A. M. Honoré (1959, p. 48) discuss mental events to the limited extent that they analyze interpersonal transactions, where one person gives another a reason for acting. J. L. Mackie (1974, chap. 5) critiques their analysis. I have already discussed Collingwood's view of the root sense of causation as motivation of an agent by an agent. But all these analyses of interpersonal transaction miss *causation as progeneration*; they concern the conditions under which one agent can be said to have given another a reason for acting but do not consider the mental processes involved in recognizing a reason or translating that reason into action. While Hart and Honoré point out such necessary conditions as that the second actor must know of and understand the significance of what the first actor has said or done, and that the second actor must form his intention after the first actor's intervention, nonetheless, the mental events involved are a black box: a reason comes in and an action comes out. The causal train as it passes through the

the mind is unseen, unknown, unanalyzed. This is both more and less clearly the case with Mackie, who, on the one hand, focuses on actions as causes in cases of interpersonal transaction ("B would not have opened the safe on this occasion, in these circumstances, if A had not threatened him" [p. 122]), but, on the other hand, does come close to mentioning that to make such statements we rely on general knowledge of mental processes ("To be able to say this, we need to know that B is not prone to open the safe gratuitously in the presence of strangers or in response to unauthoritative request" [p. 122]). Yet again, the causal train through the mind and in particular the progenerative nature of mental causation are ignored.

That theories of causation should have both ignored *causation as progeneration* and largely neglected the mind go hand in hand, for to neglect the sequence of conception, gestation, birth, and nurturing as a sequence of causation is to neglect both progeneration and a popular conception of mental operation.*

When theories about conceptions of causation have attempted to explain things human—as in the disciplines of history, law, and sociology—they focus on actions as causes, without tracing the actions back to the mental causation. Thus Hart and Honoré, speaking of law, write, "We do not trace the cause *through* the deliberate act" (p. 40) and "A deliberate human act is therefore most often a barrier and a goal in tracing back causes in such inquiries: it is something *through* which we do not trace the cause of a later event and something *to* which we do trace the cause through intervening causes of other kinds" (p. 41).

This is simply not the case in kinship metaphor, as myriad statements like "Purposelessness is the mother of crime" readily prove. On the contrary, though action is often a cause in kinship metaphors, kinship metaphors pay sharp

---

*It seems that progeneration and knowledge were conceptually linked in the evolution of Indo-European languages, too: it can be found in Pokorny (1959, pp. 373-78) that a common etymological source is shared by the group of words including progenitor, genitals, generation, genesis, kind, and kin, and the group of words including know, cunning, can, notice, and cognition.

attention to tracing behavior back to mental events, and mental events to either world situations or other mental events. Among other tracings, it takes suicide back to despair, enterprise back to hope, magnificence to ambition, evil to love of money, and gambling to avarice. In "If poverty is the mother of crimes, want of sense is the father of them," the cause is traced back past the deliberate action to both terminal mental events and mental events caused in turn by world situations. *Causation as progeneration* finds itself capable of handling thoughts, states of psychology, beliefs, and intentions, whereas *causation as action, as regularity*, and *as necessary and sufficient conditions* naturally stress actions and events.

Mental events do not seem in our conceptions to have quite the regularity, in the sense of repeated sequences, that one finds in the worlds of physics or direct manipulation. Frequently a mental event seems to be, if not *sui generis,* then at least not best explained by reference to precedents and other minds. *Causation as progeneration* finds itself particularly apt as a metaphor for singular events, hence for many mental events.

We feel that no or very little sense of necessary and sufficient conditions is involved in our mental events, in their influence on behavior and other mental events, or in the effect of the world situation on mental events. We tend to explain mental events in terms not of precise conditions but rather of indeterminate and indistinct attitudes, perceptions, mental traits, and triggering motivations.

This indeterminacy and indistinction are apt: while we can experiment with the external world and we can see what we manipulate and we can observe action directly, we have only very indeterminate and indistinct knowledge of the array of conditions of mental events. The key technique for determining them, introspection of various sorts, is inherently vague in its focus, imprecise in its discoveries, and biased in its search. *Causation as progeneration* illuminates salient conditions and marks them as having, against a background of other conditions, the power to produce, but it does not seek necessary and sufficient conditions. Indeed, it does not even presuppose that they exist or could be separated from an organic whole. This suits it for explaining mental genera-

tion. Theories of causation that neglect either mind or progeneration will neglect both, because they are coupled.

Causation as necessary and sufficient conditions has its utility in predictive power. But to account for a mental event or
to account for behavior by tracing it back to a mental event
is not inherently predictive. To show the genesis of something does not, in the realm of mind, mean that it will be
generated again. In theoretical sciences, knowing the causes
means predictability of events. In applied sciences, knowing
the causes often means ability to control the events. But neither prediction nor control is inherent in progeneration: tracing a child's parentage does not mean one can predict other
children, and it certainly does not mean that the occurrence
of future children can be controlled if one only knows the
genesis of some previous child. Since citing the causes of
mental events or the mental causes of behavior does not
inherently imply prediction or control but only explanation,
concepts of mental causation and of progeneration again fit
each other closely.

Causation as necessary and sufficient conditions—whether
illustrated by billiard balls or differential equations—naturally
suggests determinism in the sense that (1) conditions determine effects, which, as conditions, determine subsequent
effects, and so on, and (2) an effect cannot occur if the
necessary and sufficient conditions do not obtain and cannot
be prevented if they do. The acceptance of this type of causation as the ultimate explanation of events has led, when it
has occurred, to the transference of determinism to human
events. The alternatives have traditionally been statistical or
probabilistic laws in physics, and varieties of free will in
human affairs. *Causation as progeneration*, not suggesting
determinism, never leads to a conflict between (1) our concepts of causation and (2) our concept of human behavior as
the interactions of influence, feeling, thought, will, desires,
beliefs, and intentions.

When we are concerned with mental causes (or with historiography), we are often concerned not with tracing back
from an effect to a cause but rather with discovering the
consequences of something, as if to find its offspring.

Mental events involve animation and, often, will and the
power of will. We consider a mind as living and willful: the

efficacy of the mind to desire or intend or to produce mental events matches well with our conception of the efficacy, desire, will, intention, and life of a parent. This is natural: a person and a mind are close as concepts. As causes, they have will and life. But *causation as necessary and sufficient conditions* or *as regularity* concerns principally will-less events. We are reluctant to personify such will-less events. We are likewise reluctant to personify mere physical systems unless we can see them as something higher, too. Since the attribution of will or efficacy is unjustified for these systems, we seek to explain them by reference not to intention but rather to sequences, to predictable patterns, to the order and integrity of a known structure. We then do not have to grant efficacy to the order or structure. But we have no difficulty anthropomorphizing minds.

As I mentioned before, there seem commonly to be three main ways to model systems conceptually. The first is in terms of something like the physics of the system—in terms of its elements and the laws governing them, as for electrical circuits, celestial motion, photon emission, osmosis, the kinesis of gas. The second is in terms of the components of the system and their intended functioning. For example, consider the human body or a house. Each has components with functions, and the functions are combined into larger functions. Each component operates or performs, and we concern ourselves with that performance. To explain the system, we refer not to its physics or to laws which it must obey but rather to the functions of its components. When the body has kidney malfunction or the floor of the house begins to slope, we conclude that the system is not functioning properly and seek to locate the malfunctioning components. We certainly do not conclude that the body is violating laws of physics (the kidney, even malfunctioning, is perfectly in line with the laws of physics) or that the house is violating the laws of physics (the sagging foundation is in fact a textbook illustration of deformation under forces). But we say that something has gone wrong with the componential structure. We refer back to the componential or functional model of the system and conclude that the kidney is malfunctioning and will have to be treated or removed, and that some of the foundations are rotten and will have to be replaced.

The third way is by personification, or, more generally, by attributing to something components of intelligent animated beings, like beliefs, desires, intentions, goals, plans, psychological states, powers, and will. We model not only people this way but also some cosmic forces, most mammals and institutions, a few intelligent mechanisms or machines, and even lesser animals. We say, "The gods were jealous," "Exxon is just being greedy," "Whiskers tore up the couch because she was angry at being left alone," "The computer wiped out my buffer," and "The cockroaches, under cover of darkness, headed for the plate of butter until the light flicked back on, whereupon they froze to avoid detection, but scattered when they sensed the bundled magazine swinging in the air."

Now, science looks principally at the first way of modeling (elements and laws), and peripherally at the second way (components and functions), but very little at all at the third way of modeling (anthropomorphism, or, as Daniel Dennett would call it, "adopting an intentional stance"). Modeling by anthropomorphism, frequent in our discussions of psychology, history, indeed anything human and many more things besides, has been largely ignored by the theoretical natural sciences and their applications. Science, in brief, usually ignores mind. Of course, it sometimes proposes that the third and second ways of modeling can be traced back to the first; anthropomorphic models can be mapped into scientific models. Whatever the truth of that, the insight is usually of little help because the very things we are interested in explaining when we are modeling by anthropomorphism— that is, intention, belief, will, efficacy, and so on—are lost in the reduction.

This is why theories about concepts of causation are so far removed from the arts, certainly from poetry: they ignore the kind of causation we often use to understand biology, life, and the mind. When we attribute components of mind and will to a system, our understanding of its operation very often relies on *causation as progeneration*. We are concerned with progeneration in the mind, and of this, science tells us nothing. The poetry of love and fear, of ideals and disappointment, the literary traditions of vision, prophecy, contemplation, and self-analysis, the psychological facts not only of will and belief and intention but also of aesthetics and

artistic invention—all this involves *causation as progeneration.*
And all this the theoretical and applied natural sciences do
not touch, and theories of causation as regularity, as necessary and sufficient conditions, as action or manipulation,
either ignore or slight. *Causation as efficacy* suits modeling
by anthropomorphism.

As a final unifying example, consider again literary and
linguistic production—from a spontaneous witticism in
conversation to a lyric poem. We all have conceptual models
of this kind of causation, and in these models, conception,
gestation, birth, and nurturing are techniques of causing a
thing to exist. The omnipresence of such models and the
range of their application argue for the recognition of *causation as progeneration* as a basic concept of causation.

4.8 Definitions and causal generalizations

What does *causation as progeneration* tell us about the onto-
logical status of causes and effects? To discuss this, I need to
distinguish four related concepts: indeterminacy, indistinction, general terms, and causal generalization.

"Indeterminacy" concerns cases where part of a concept is
fuzzy in someone's understanding, but he believes that the
concept is not fuzzy in reality. Indeterminacy, he would say,
results from ignorance, sometimes incorrigible ignorance. I
may believe that a subatomic particle has a position and a
momentum at a fixed time but also that I cannot determine
both accurately. My concept of the particle is indeterminate,
but I believe that in reality the position and momentum of
the particle are well-defined. Or, I have a concept of the
rings of Saturn or Uranus, lack (and believe everyone else
lacks) data on their stability, yet believe that there exists a
clear and well-defined truth to the matter. My concept of
these rings is fuzzy, but I might believe that in reality the
rings are well-defined.

"Indistinction" concerns cases where the fuzziness of a
concept is a deliberate fuzziness, where someone prefers not
to define parts of a concept, even though he might have the
power to do so. For example, I have a concept of greater
Los Angeles as a geographical area. But, in this concept, the

border is not precise, and I prefer it so. If you ask me to draw a border on a map, I will, and if you then draw a border a little closer or farther, I will admit that either of those will serve just as well. I prefer not to have certain parts of certain singular concepts defined, and then to be held to the definitions. I prefer them fuzzy.

"General term" means many things. It might be argued that giving one singular identity to any two concepts, or one singular identity to an indeterminate concept and hence all its potentialities, or one singular identity to an indistinct concept and hence all its acceptable specifications, all involve general terms and generalizations. Yes. But I would like to give generalization only two senses here: (1) where one term can be applied to more than one singular concept, and (2) where a causal generalization is being made (e.g., "guns cause death"). The first I will refer to as "general terms" and the second as "causal generalization."

What does *causation as progeneration* have to teach us about generalization, indistinction, and indeterminacy? Let us begin with singular causal statements, cases where both cause and effect are singular concepts, as in:

George Washington is the father of his country.

Elizabeth was a child of the Italian Renaissance.

Thomas Carlyle is in spirit a child of the great revolution.

Consider also a few examples where only one of the cause and effect is a singular concept:

Babylon is the mother of harlots and abominations.

The moon is the mother of pathos and pity.

England is the mother of Parliaments.

So is she that cometh the mother of songs.

The main point to be made about these statements, a point directly derived from the progenerative nature of the causality involved and conflicting trenchantly with *causation as necessary and sufficient conditions*, is that in representations of causation, there can be great utility in indistinct concepts, and either utility or no harm in indeterminate concepts. Though *causation as necessary and sufficient conditions* seeks causation in the precise location of causal conditions, their precise definition, and, importantly, their separation from what is not causal, kinship metaphors involving *causation as progeneration* not only ignore but also outrightly reject this distinction and determinacy. The "I" which is the "child of the modern era," for instance, is indeterminate. One lacks, perhaps incorrigibly, complete knowledge of one's mind. Yet this indeterminacy of effect in no way impedes the assertion of causality. Importantly, it is not merely that there are indeterminate parts of "I" that are somehow not involved in the causal statement. No. There are parts of "I" that, though perhaps indeterminate, are quite clearly progenerated by the modern age. *Determinacy of cause and effect is not necessary for ascription of causality.* This sounds strange only because it challenges the ascendant views of how human beings understand causation. Specification of concepts is not necessary for the perception of their causal relationship. The "modern era" is an indistinct concept and preferred as such. We have a sense that fuller determination, though enlightening, would not alter the fact of progenerative causation, and that sharp distinction might be not only unnecessary but also unwarranted and unmotivated. It would not have any conceptual utility, and the wrong distinction might render the statement of causality less true.

Indistinct and indeterminate concepts are highly useful in understanding and expressing causation. We can feel that we know *that* causality is involved, without having worked out *how* causality is involved, perhaps without even having the sense that a reductive knowledge can be obtained. This suggests that the criteria used for feeling that one knows *that* are not necessarily the possession of knowledge *how* or even the certainty of its attainability. With causation, the criterion for judging *that* causality applies is often the perception of an efficacy in the cause to produce, accompanied by the production. The exact workings of this efficacy may be another matter altogether, may not in fact be knowable. Knowing *that* causality is involved does not require knowing *how*. Often, indeterminate and indistinct terms allow us to express that we know *that*, without committing us to knowing *how*.

People could not operate efficiently if they required themselves always to know *how*, first because knowing *how* requires great analysis and time, second because this kind of knowledge is often unattainable. The other varieties of causation previously discussed require often that the understander know *how*. *Causation as progeneration* requires much less knowing *how*, sometimes only a knowledge *that*. To determine and distinguish concepts is to work toward knowing *how*. Since this knowledge is often not the goal of *causation as progeneration*; since the wrong distinction might render the knowledge *that* untrue; and since often there is no sense that reduction to specified components is possible, *causation as progeneration* often prefers fuzziness or indistinction and views indeterminacy as insignificant.

Sometimes we inspect a theorem to be proved or a line of poetry to be understood, or listen to what someone is trying to tell us, and we have a sense that we understand long before we work out the details of the understanding or even know whether those details can be isolated. What is happening in these cases? Perhaps when we try to understand, we seek methods of understanding to apply, and there are constraints on the application of these methods. When these constraints are met, the method has been accessed but not yet used. These feelings of understanding result from successfully accessing methods before using them. On one hand, sometimes we feel that we know *that* something or other, but we turn out to be mistaken, in which case we may modify the constraints on the methods. On the other hand, it is likely that we can simultaneously access many more methods of understanding than we can use in parallel. So we have the feeling that this type of understanding is somehow fuller and more holistic than analytic understanding. When we follow one thread, we lose sight of the weave to which it belongs.

In statements of the form "x = kinship-term of y" that involve *causation*, we employ another kind of indistinction. Relatively sketchy representations of x and y and of possible metaphoric inferences of the kinship term can be used. Locating a plausible metaphoric inference helps direct the exploration of x and y. Exploring components of x and y helps deepen the metaphoric inference. So we can work down, through levels of indistinction, into the details to locate components important to the understanding. This is very far from the notion of a causal statement as presenting the conditions necessary and sufficient for the causation of the precisely named effect. Consider "So is she that cometh the mother of songs" and "Night is the mother of despair." The more detailed parts of "she" must be inspected to locate the potential component of the concept "she" that indicates power to inspire art. The more detailed parts of "night" must be inspected to locate the potential components of night that might engender despair: prototypically, people are asleep at night; one is alone; diverting activity is absent; the vitality of sunlight is missing; vision is limited; one's environment contracts. A writer presenting any such statements is not at all presenting conditions necessary and sufficient to produce effects, nor is he implying regularity in some sequence.

Causation as regularity sees all causation as generalization over sequences. The singular causal statements we have considered refute the notion of causation as a generalization of a regularity. These singular causal statements cannot be handled by Hume's conception of *causation as regularity*, and they refute Mill's notion of the common sense of causation as "invariable and unconditional sequence." No regular sequence, much less one invariable or unconditional, is contained in "George Washington is the father of his country" or "Elizabeth was the child of the Italian Renaissance." Kinship metaphors agree with Mackie that "it is easy to refute the claim that a singular causal statement normally implies a simple regularity statement, of the form that instances of a certain kind of event are always, or even often, followed by instances of another kind of event: the taking of a contraceptive pill may cause one woman's death although millions of women have taken large numbers of exactly similar pills and survived" (p. 77).

Even when general terms and causal generalizations occur in kinship metaphors implying causation, they have no necessary connection at all with invariability, and are not intended as predictive. To say "Night is the mother of annoyance sad" or "Night is the mother of despair" or "Despair is the mother of madness" or "The moon is the mother of pathos and pity" or "Dreams are the children of an Idle Brane" in no way implies invariability or predictability of effect. Their purpose rather is to locate a latent efficacy in the cause to produce the effect.

There are traditional problems with general terms occurring in causal generalizations. When are two causes or two sets of conditions sufficiently similar to be captured by a general term in a causal generalization? Which similarities between the two causes or two sets of conditions are indispensable, which dispensable? These problems disappear under *causation as progeneration*. One need only be concerned that the general term can be applied linguistically to all the concepts one wishes to include and that causes have the latent efficacy to produce the effect. *Causation as progeneration* can find indistinction in general terms preferable, and indeterminacy no detriment.

4.9 Summary

There is a type of causal statement that cannot be accounted for by any of the usual notions of how we conceive of causation. We have the conceptual metaphor CAUSATION IS PROGENERATION, and the characteristics of this conceptual metaphor match those needed to account for this type of causal statement. It seems natural to conclude therefore that we understand this otherwise unaccounted-for type of causal statement by virtue of the conceptual metaphor CAUSATION IS PROGENERATION. An abstractionist explanation of these observations must conform to my main point that we use some concept very like *causation as progeneration* to understand these statements and nevertheless must still be wrong because it cannot account for the asymmetry in the mapping between causation and progeneration.

No one of our conceptions of causation is *the* basis for the others. We conceive of them all as varieties of one concept, causation, not because the conceptions resemble each other, but because we use them all cognitively for the similar purpose of accounting for how something comes to be.

Causation as progeneration is the main conception of causation we use to understand mental creation.

As *causation as progeneration* shows, indistinct and indeterminate definitions and causal generalizations are often useful and accurate, and the attempt to define concepts or to express causal generalizations in terms of analytic traditions is, from the stance of *causation as progeneration*, misconceived.

APPENDIX

Lucretius on causation:

The first principle of our study we will derive from this, that no thing is ever by divine power produced from nothing. For assuredly a dread holds all mortals thus in bond, because they behold many things happening in heaven and earth whose causes they can by no means see, and they think them to be done by divine power. For which reasons, when we shall perceive that nothing can be created from nothing, then we shall at once more correctly understand from that principle what we are seeking, both the source from which each thing can be made and the manner in which everything is done without the working of gods.

For if things came out of nothing, all kinds of things could be produced from all things, nothing would want a seed. Firstly, men could arise from the sea, from the earth scaly tribes, and birds could hatch from the sky; cattle and other farm animals and every kind of wild creature would fill desert and cultivated land alike, with no certainty as to birth. Nor would trees be constant in bearing the same fruit, but they would interchange: all would be able to bear all. Seeing that there would be no bodies apt to generate each kind, how could there be a constant unchanging mother for things? But as it is, because every kind is produced from fixed seeds, the source of everything that is born and comes forth into the borders of light is that in which is the material of it and its first bodies; and therefore it is impossible that all things be born from all things, because in particular things resides a distinct power.

(principium cuius hinc nobis exordia sumet,/ nullam rem e nilo gigni divinitus umquam./ quippe ita formido mortalis

continet omnis,/ quod multa in terris fieri caeloque tuentur/
quorum operum causas nulla ratione videre/ possunt, ac fieri
divino numine rentur./ quas ob res ubi viderimus nil posse
creari/ de nilo, tum quod sequimur iam rectius inde/ perspi-
ciemus, et unde queat res quaeque creari/ et quo quaeque
modo fiant opera sine divom./ Nam si de nilo fierent, ex
omnibu' rebus/ omne genus nasci posset, nil semine egeret./
e mare primum homines, e terra posset oriri/ squamigerum
genus et volucres erumpere caelo;/ armenta atque aliae
pecudes, genus omne ferarum,/ incerto partu culta ac deserta
tenerent;/ nec fructus idem arboribus constare solerent,/ sed
mutarentur: ferre omnes omnia possent./ quippe ubi non
essent genitalia corpora cuique,/ qui posset mater rebus con-
sistere certa?/ at nunc seminibus quia certis quaeque crean-
tur,/ inde enascitur atque oras in luminis exit/ materies ubi
inest cuiusque et corpora prima;/ atque hac re nequeunt ex
omnibus omnia gigni,/ quod certis in rebus inest secreta
facultas.) (*De Rerum Natura*, 1.149-73. Text and translation
from Rouse)

5   *Similarity*

I have discussed how we understand many sorts of concepts in terms of kinship. In general, what does it mean to understand one domain in terms of another? One popular answer to this very general question is that we sometimes understand that two domains are *similar*. We say that the source and target domains share similar features or structures, and so the target can be understood in terms of the source.

If someone tells us that two domains are similar, how do we go about trying to understand their similarity? Can the way kinship metaphor uses the sibling relation to indicate similarity give us elaborate insight into how we understand similarity, as the way it uses the progenerative relation to indicate causation gives us (as I have claimed) elaborate insight into how we conceive of causation?

No, not at all. The parent-child relation is ubiquitous and rich in our models of kinship and in kinship metaphors. Lateral relations are relatively secondary. Still, the use of these lateral relations in kinship metaphors will let me tease out a few specific, exploratory assertions about how we try to understand that two concepts are similar.

To do this, I must distinguish again between creative and noncreative metaphors. To understand a creative metaphor, we have to reconceive, in some way, the target domain. The metaphor thus creates meaning. It might, for instance, create similarity. To understand a noncreative metaphor, we do not have to reconceive the target domain. We might, for instance, understand it as asking us to locate features or structures already shared in our conceptual models of the source and target domains. I will say we understand a metaphor noncreatively when we do not revise our mental conceptions and creatively when we do.

When we try to understand a metaphor creatively or noncreatively, how do we know which connections to look for and which to ignore? If someone says "John is a middle-aged baby," how do we know not to understand this as saying that John wears diapers and sucks on bottles? Context can guide us as we go looking for similarity. What do we do in the absence of explicit guidance from the context?

My key contention here is that, in the absence of contextual prompts to do otherwise, a reader seeks to match the two concepts involved in a metaphor noncreatively by comparing the stereotypical behaviors of the two concepts. By behavior I mean how a thing operates. Music and poetry, for example, have behaviors: they both give sequences of sounds and affect minds through the aural sense.

Many concepts presented in English as substantives, as nouns, are cognitively represented, prototypically, as behaviors of something or someone. "Death," for instance, may have a sophisticated cognitive representation as "the cessation of organismic functions," but prototypically the cognitive representation is "the behavior of a dead thing." Similarly, sleep is commonly the behavior of a sleeping thing, humility is the behavior of a humble person, and so on.

Just as there are stereotypical concepts of things, so are there stereotypical behaviors. For example, the stereotypical behavior of someone sleeping is to do nothing and notice nothing while lying down with eyes temporarily closed. Attached to this idealized cognitive model are details, potential instances, and even corrections. For example, attached to our stereotype of sleeping is the correction that the sleeper is not actually doing nothing, that he has normal metabolic functions, that he might dream, that he may notice things unconsciously.

Kinship metaphors seem to indicate that a reader tries first to match the stereotypical behaviors of the two concepts (if they have behaviors). A behavior might be thought of as having certain stereotypical components: actions, states of being, relations among the actions and states of being, and conditions on the actions and states. An action might be thought of as having stereotypical components such as agents, objects, locations, instruments, and so on.

Matching of behaviors compares the values of stereotypical components. Thus since music gives a sequence of notes affecting minds through the aural sense and poetry gives a sequence of words affecting minds through the aural sense, their stereotypical behaviors match but for the value of the component "material": sounds versus words. By performing this match, we understand "Music is twin-sister to poetry."

Consider "After Glotonye thanne comth Lecherie, for these two synnes been so ny cosyns that ofte tyme they wol nat departe." Suppose we have representations of gluttony and lechery as behaviors that consist of an action of getting and of conditions of repetition and excess but that differ on the object of the getting. Then we can understand the similarity by matching behavior.

Sleep and Death represented as behaviors of inactivity and unconsciousness can be matched to understand "Sleep, Death's twin brother."

Cant and Hypocrisy represented as the deceitful misrepresentation of components of the mind can be matched to understand the phrase "Cant is the twin sister of hypocrisy."

Accuracy represented as any behavior (including expression) which is true to some standard, and honesty represented as behavior (usually expression) which is true to one's knowledge, can be matched to understand "Accuracy is the twin brother of honesty."

A boaster, represented as one who misrepresents in words by emphasizing his assets, and a liar, represented as one who misrepresents in words, can be matched to understand "A boaster and a liar are cousins."

Someone stricken with the plague behaves in a certain manner, with certain symptoms, particularly a virulent and consumptive fever. Someone stricken with another disease may have this same main symptom. This is how we understand "Other diseases, neere cousins to the plague."

One who is prejudiced and one who is illiberal both act with ungenerous narrow-mindedness, whereas one who is humble and one who is meek both act with deference and without self-assertion; hence "Prejudice is the twin of illiberality" and "Humility, with its twin sister meekness."

My second claim concerns the case where a reader cannot match noncreatively the behaviors of two concepts. Suppose that one concept is exclusively behavioral but the other is not, so that sheer partial matching of behavior is not possible. In this case, kinship metaphors seem to indicate that the reader seeks to determine whether the behavior implied for the nonbehavioral term is in fact possible and fitting. If so, the reader accepts that implication as an understanding; he maps the behavior onto the nonbehavioral concept.

Consider "The Sophist is the cousin of the parasite and the flatterer." "Parasite" and "flatterer" are strictly behavioral concepts, whereas "Sophist" is a membership term, with many potential behaviors attached. We understand by implication: we see the Sophist's behavior with his auditors as the behavior of flattery and parasitism; that is, he flatters his auditors in order to derive a living from them.

This example also illustrates that, in marginal cases, implication is from the more clearly behavioral concept to the less clearly behavioral concept, and, in general, implication is from the more specific concept to the less specific concept.

Consider as examples of implication of behavior from more specific to less specific concept the following:

[Of the linnet:]
My dazzled sight he oft deceives,
A brother of the dancing leaves.

[Of a person:]
Ah, brother of the brief but blazing star!

We are told that the leaves are dancing: we see their stereotypical behavior as flitting, fluttering, glancing light, moving rhythmically. The metaphor implies that this behavior applies to the bird. Similarly, we are told that the star is brief but blazing: we see its stereotypical behavior as shining briefly but intensely. The metaphor implies that this behavior applies to the person.

Consider "Now wyll I proue ye a lyar / Next cosyne to a friar." "Liar" is strictly a behavior-concept, while "friar" is a membership-concept. So the implication is from liar to friar.

(An implication from friar to liar might also be contradicted by the reader's real-world knowledge.) A liar stereotypically speaks falsehoods to others to deceive them and probably to manipulate them. We are to see the behavior of a friar as the behavior of a liar.

My third claim is that when we match nonbehavioral concepts, we do so by certain operations on idealized cognitive models. These operations are:

(1) Understanding that the two concepts are two instances of the same idealized cognitive model, implicitly distinguished—if they are components of physical reality—by space and time:

> That April Morn, of this the very brother
>
> Hark how the Bells upon the waters play
> Their Sister-tunes, from Thames his either side.
>
> The days of life are sisters.

Why is it that two April mornings are seen as closer than, say, poetry and music, especially when the April mornings could be very different, and the poetry might be designed to be sung as music? It is because two instances of one idealized cognitive model that differ only in space-time location will always be seen as closer than two different idealized cognitive models.

(2) Understanding that the two concepts are two instances of the same idealized cognitive model, distinguished implicitly—if components of physical reality—by space and time, and explicitly by named differences.

> Mt. Olivet overtopping its sister, Mt. Moriah, three hundred feet
>
> A clear stream flowing with a muddy one, / Till in its wayward current it absorbs / . . . The vexed eddies of its wayward brother
>
> Hawthorn Hall was not first cousin to the Aspens, having nothing of the villa about it.
>
> Heere's the twyn brother of thy Letter.

The two mountains differ on names and height; the two streams on clarity; the two buildings on grandeur; the two letters (one knows from context) only on names.

(3) Understanding that two idealized cognitive models share the same immediate supercategory.

> I am the little woodlark. / The skylark is my cousin. (Supercategory = lark)

> There should you behold a Mine of Tynne, sister to Silver. (Supercategory = shiny metal)

> The art of roasting or rather broiling, which I take to be the elder brother (Supercategory = cooking)

> If carnal Death (the younger brother) doe / Usurpe the body, our soule, which subject is / To th'elder death, by sinne, is freed by this. (Supercategory = death)

> Time, pleased with your triumphs o'er his brother Space (Supercategory = parameter of physical reality)

> The sun's pale sister, drawn by magic strain (Supercategory = prominent heavenly body)

> Soon—as when summer of his sister spring / Crushes and tears the rare enjewelling. (Supercategory = season)

We have less confidence that generalizing to supercategory achieves a match as the number of necessary generalizations increases. For instance, one is satisfied that a tiger, a jaguar, and a panther are alike in that they are all big cats; we need to generalize only one step to a common supercategory. But we are not satisfied, if asked how a cow, a snake, and a rose are alike, to claim that they are all alive, though we may be forced to that answer. The supercategory is too many steps up.

(4) Understanding that similarity is asserted, but that the similarity is explicit and highlighted, and not to be supplied by the reader:

> Sparta in laws and institutions is the sister of Crete.

(5) Understanding that two concepts have the same psychological progenitor, as in "In vain am driven on false hope, hope sister of despair." Sharing a psychological progenitor can cohere with having similar behaviors, as in "A boaster and a liar are cousins."

The reader may also understand that the two concepts are grouped concomitants. *Grouping* does not imply similarity, though *similarity* and *grouping* often cohere, as in "The sun's pale sister, drawn by magic strain," or "Cant is the twin sister of hypocrisy."

Research on similarity has become popular, but very little is known, and what remains unknown will have to be treated extensively as a subject in its own right. The few insights provided here by kinship metaphor tell us little more than that research into similarity has only just begun. For example, two popular theories, by Dedre Gentner (1980, 1983) and Jaime Carbonell (1981), are trenchantly contradicted by the evidence from kinship metaphor.

Gentner claims that metaphoric mappings map objects in the source domain onto objects in the target domain, that relations between objects in the source domain are preserved in the mapping, but that attributes of objects are usually not preserved or mapped. As Gentner (1983) puts it, "analogy is characterized by the mapping of relations between objects, rather than attributes of objects." This characterization of metaphor as a structure-preserving isomorphism in the algebraic sense is untrue to kinship metaphor, because kinship metaphor constantly preserves attributes like behavior and rarely maps between domains anything like algebraic structures. Gentner prefers to look at metaphors involving the solar system as a source domain. Her notion of metaphor as an algebraic structure-mapping may fit such metaphors but not others.

Carbonell has argued that we construct analogies to help us solve problems that are of interest to us, and so we try to understand an analogy as offering help in understanding a problem: "Solutions to problems generated by metaphors are ONLY useful as heuristic problem-solving advice." Again, this does not apply where kinship is the source domain. Kinship metaphor often matches behaviors that have nothing to do with goals or plans.

The failure of these theories to account for kinship metaphor suggests that the nature and purpose of metaphor may vary with source domain and target domain, which is to say with the meaning-content of the metaphor.

6   *Genealogy*

The explicit short kinship metaphors I have presented show some of the ways we use genealogy as a basis for conceptual metaphors. I would now like to suggest how widely and powerfully we use genealogy in other conceptual metaphors.

Genealogy underlies our concepts of diachronic and synchronic classification. Linguistic derivation across time is expressed in terms of parentage, and the consequent classification of languages is expressed in terms of families, descent, and relation. Classification as genealogy appears not merely in the well-known taxonomic classification of biology by reference to family structure but also in the Aristotelian doctrine (*Categories*) that all descriptive expressions fall into a few overlapping but exhaustive classes. Genealogy underlies these classes: they are said to be the highest *genera;* any other category falls below one of them as a *species*. Further, for Aristotle, genealogy underlies classification, which underlies definitions, which, as "the first principles of demonstration," lead us to "all scientific knowledge" (*Posterior Analytics*, 90b). Modern theories of categorization that overthrow many classical principles of categorization do so not by abandoning the basic genealogical metaphor but rather by analyzing and emphasizing our conception of *family resemblance* (see Wittgenstein 1958 and Rosch 1977).

The concept of relation derives from genealogy, among other things. A is the son of B, and C the son of D: son-

hood is abstracted as a relation, and the structures of the
pairs A-B and C-D compared.

Such comparison suggests the concept of a *homomorphism*.
A *homomorphism* is a mapping of one set into another in
such a way as to preserve *relations*. Any two kinship trees
suggest the abstract concept of partial homomorphism,
because the core of one tree can be mapped onto the core of
the other tree by mapping the ego-node of the first onto the
ego-node of the second and each lineal ancestor to the
corresponding ancestor. This mapping will preserve relations. It is by recognizing (partial) homomorphisms that we
recognize shared structure in the world, in our cognitive
models, and in our language.

That all actual kinship trees are partially homomorphic in
this way means that all must share a common minimal structure. This minimal structure can be extended in systematic
ways. Each actual kinship tree is thus an instance, an
extended copy, of an abstract kinship tree. This yields the
Platonist notion, underlying so much of our everyday and
scientific theory, of the unseen model and its copies, of ideal
definition and individual predications, of generalizations and
their instances.

In this abstract model of a kinship tree, offspring are distinguished by sex and precedence. Any node can be related
to any other node by following the path through intermediary nodes. The set of paths between node A and node B is
disjoint from the set of paths between node C and node D
unless A equals B and C equals D, in which case the two sets
are identical. More, if there is a relationship (path) between
B and C, and a relationship (path) between A and B, this
defines a relationship (path) between A and C. Also, relations compose associatively: that is, given A, B, C, and D, we
can (1) join the paths from A to B and B to C, and then join
the result to the path from C to D, or (2) join the paths from
B to C and C to D, and then join the path from A to B to
the result. It is the same either way. In sum, we can derive
from genealogy the ideas that (1) any two elements of the set
stand in some relation, (2) relations compose, and (3) the
ultimate composed relation is not dependent on the order in
which one composes pairs in a fixed string. In fact, a kinship
tree, whereupon we define the morphisms of a node A onto

a node B as the paths between them, is a structure called a *category* by mathematicians. The concept of a category, a general superstructure in algebra, underlies the mathematics of types of structure. Genealogy, an idealized kinship tree, is in the mathematical sense a model of a category.

Kinship relations give, as I mentioned in chapter 1, our closest metaphors for metaphor itself. More accurately, if the concept of metaphor is the target domain, kinship is the best source domain for understanding it. We expect kin standing in a given relation to fit one of the stereotypical partial homomorphisms that attach to that relation. We expect them to be similar and dissimilar in one of a limited number of stereotypical ways. Generations produce a kind of living anaphora: from parent to child we see repetition and variation, similarity and difference.

Perhaps most profoundly, our recognition of similarity and resemblance often refuses to be reduced to a listing of shared and different attributes, to a tabulation of discrete elements, or to a model of distinct elements and precise relations. The fuzziness of resemblance fits well our notion of family resemblance.

There are many understandings of time: as a cycle, as overlapping cycles, as a river, and so on. The prevailing understanding of time in Western culture is based on the representation of time as a line, and it seems to be the concept of genealogy that accounts for this relation between space and time. A genealogy is a lineage, a line, conceived of spatially, yet the line is a time line, a spatial conceptualization of chronology. Although the repetition in nature of the cycles of the moon or the sun can yield the concept of a clock based on intervals and recursion, it does not yield the concept of irretrievable aging. But biology does: biological things age. And neither natural repetition nor mere biological aging yields the concept of the irretrievable passage of linear time. But lineage does: it branches irretrievably forward, so that a person, even after death, moves irretrievably backward in the genealogy. First one is, say, a son, then a father, then a grandfather, and so on ever backward. This is genealogy and not simply biology, for although biological transformation can yield the concept of age, yet it does not indicate a succession of linear ages. And though natural cycles can indicate change and recursion, yet we have no understanding that today's spring is the chronological descendant of last spring, no unification of time as a series of sequential generations, except by reference to a genealogical tree.

Genealogy connects past, present, and future into one. It connects ancestors in the past to real descendants in the present and potential descendants in the future, binds them into one living unit. This yields a model of humanity that unifies human diversity: living individuals are a lateral plurality, vastly divergent, even competing, but nonetheless united vertically into a descending tree.

Many of the seemingly intuitive aspects of kinship as conceptual metaphor can be precisely understood by reference to the synthetic theory of evolution, to genetics. If one thinks in terms of the descent of genes or genotypes rather than persons, then descendants are quite literally partial physical copies of ancestors. There are specific genetic mechanisms in the stages of transmission for variation and similarity. The individual embodies his ancestors concretely. Each stereotypical relation—of similarity, inheritance, variation, partition, and so on—between kin has its analogue in the more exact but less practical language of genetics.

Science models systems so that we can recognize, explain, and predict them. The conceptual metaphors implicit in our language are a kind of science. It might be said that genetic laws of transmission or the sociobiological principle of inclusive fitness make sense out of metaphors in language based on metaphoric inferences like *inheritance* or *functional property transfer*, but the influence really works in the reverse order: it is the earlier formulation of these sciences in the metaphors of thought and language that made their scientific formulations seem conceptually so natural.

7   *Conclusion*

Members of a language community share many things,
including conceptual systems, cognitive processes, and every
aspect of a common language. This common cognitive
apparatus permits them to have a literature. It includes a
few basic conceptual metaphors that use kinship as their
source domain.

These basic metaphors interact with our commonplace
notions, with other basic metaphors, and with basic metonymies to yield ten major conceptual metaphoric inference
patterns. I have named them *property transfer, similarity,
group, inheritance, components and contents, order and succession, causation as progeneration, biological resource as parent,
place and time as parent,* and *lineage in the world, the mind,
and behavior.*

Some combination of these conceptual inference patterns
accounts for every one of the indefinitely many specific kinship metaphors in our language. These conceptual metaphors, metonymies, and metaphoric inference patterns are
moreover extremely rich and powerful in our thought. For
example, *lineage* reveals that we hold a conceptual model of
the paths by which things in the world, the mind, and
behavior can spring from each other. We use this model to
understand and produce language about events in the world
and the mind. CAUSATION IS PROGENERATION, a basic conceptual metaphor, allows us to understand and talk about a
wide range of important phenomena. It is our principal

conceptual tool for understanding mental invention. And our concept of genealogy also underlies our understanding of similarity, classification, linguistic derivation, relation, structure, ideals and instances, and time.

Literary authors often explain things in terms of kinship. When they do, they rely upon this shared conceptual apparatus. Milton uses kinship to conduct and present an elaborate investigation of sin and death. Blake uses it to conduct and present an elaborate investigation of the nature of human psychology and the relations between its components. To account for such literary texts requires accounting for the common conceptual and linguistic apparatus that makes them possible.

As language and literature lead us to contemplate problems in human understanding, so the study of mind turns wisely for clues to the oldest and most abiding arts. This book derives from the dual nature of literature and the human mind as doors into each other. I hope it has demonstrated the indispensability of uniting our investigations of literature, semantics, and cognition. I believe the future of such a unification could be powerful, rich, and exciting.

Bibliography

Alston, William P. 1964. *Philosophy of Language.* Englewood Cliffs, N.J.: Prentice-Hall.

Anscombe, G. E. M. 1971. *Causality and Determination.* London: Cambridge University Press.

Ayer, A. J. 1956. *The Problem of Knowledge.* Baltimore: Penguin.

Barthes, Roland. 1972. *Mythologies.* Trans. Annette Lavers. New York: Hill and Wang.

————. *S/Z.* Trans. Richard Miller. New York: Hill and Wang.

Beardsley, Monroe C. 1958. *Aesthetics.* New York: Harcourt, Brace.

————. Metaphor. In Paul Edwards, ed., *The Encyclopedia of Philosophy.* New York: Macmillan and The Free Press.

Bennett, Jonathan. 1974. Counterfactuals and Possible Worlds. *Canadian Journal of Philosophy* 4:381-402.

Berlin, Brent, Dennis E. Breedlove, and Peter H. Raven. 1974. *Principles of Tzeltal Plant Classification.* New York: Academic Press.

Black, Max. 1956. Why Cannot an Effect Precede its Cause? *Analysis* 16:49-58.

————. 1962. *Models and Metaphors.* Ithaca, N.Y.: Cornell University Press.

Blake, William, 1965. *Poetry and Prose.* Ed. D. V. Erdman. Garden City, N.Y.: Doubleday.

————. 1978. *William Blake's Writings.* Ed. G. E. Bentley, Jr. Oxford: Clarendon Press.

Blessington, Francis C. 1979. *Paradise Lost and the Classical Epic.* Boston: Routledge and Kegan Paul.

Booth, Wayne. 1974. *A Rhetoric of Irony*. Chicago: University of Chicago Press.

Brand, Myles, ed. 1976. *The Nature of Causation*. Urbana: University of Illinois Press.

Broadbent, J. B. 1967. *Some Graver Subject: An Essay on Paradise Lost*. New York: Schocken Books.

Brooke-Rose, Christine. 1965. *A Grammar of Metaphor*. London: Mercury.

Brugman, Claudia. 1981. Story of *Over*. Master's Thesis, University of California, Berkeley. Available from the Indiana University Linguistics Club, Bloomington, Indiana.

————. 1983. Extensions of Body-part Terms to Locating Expressions in Chalcatongo Mixtec. In Report No. 4 of the Survey in California and Other Indian Languages, pp. 235-290. University of California, Berkeley.

Bunge, Mario. 1959. *Causality: The Place of the Causal Principle in Modern Science*. Cambridge, Mass.: Harvard University Press.

Buchanan, Scott. 1929. *Poetry and Mathematics*. New York: John Day.

Carbonell, Jaime G. 1980. Invariance Hierarchies in Metaphor Interpretation. *Proceedings of the Third Annual Conference of the Cognitive Science Society*, pp. 292-95. Berkeley: Cognitive Science Society.

Casad, Eugene. 1982. Cora Locationals and Structured Imagery. Ph.D. diss., University of California, San Diego.

Casad, Eugene, and Ronald Langacker. 1985. "Inside" and "Outside" in Cora Grammar. *International Journal of American Linguistics* 51.3:247-81.

Chisholm, Roderick M. 1946. The Contrary-to-fact Conditional. *Mind* 55:289-307.

Chisholm, R. M., and R. Taylor. 1960. Making Things to Have Happened. *Analysis* 20:73-78.

Collingwood, R. G. 1940. *An Essay on Metaphysics*. Oxford: Clarendon.

Craig, Colette, ed. 1985. *Noun Classes*. Philadelphia: Benjamins North America.

Dennett, Daniel C. 1978. *Brainstorms: Philosophical Essays on Mind and Psychology*. Cambridge, Mass.: MIT Press.

Derrida, Jacques. 1976. *Of Grammatology*. Trans. Gayatri Chakravorty Spivak. Baltimore: Johns Hopkins University Press.

Dobbins, Austin. 1975. *Milton and the Book of Revelation: The Heavenly Cycle*. University: University of Alabama Press.

Downing, P. B. 1958. Subjunctive Conditionals, Time Order, and Causation. *Proceedings of the Aristotelian Society* 59:125-40.

Dray, William. 1959. Taylor and Chisholm on Making Things to Have Happened. *Analysis* 20:79-82.

Dummett, A. E. 1954. Can an Effect Precede its Cause? *Proceedings of the Aristotelian Society*, supplement, 28:27-44.

Dummett, Michael. 1964. Bringing About the Past. *Philosophical Review* 73:338-59.

Empson, William. 1965. *Milton's God*. London: Chatto and Windus.

Fauconnier, Gilles. 1985. *Mental Spaces*. Cambridge, Mass.: MIT Press.

Ferry, Anne. 1963. *Milton's Epic Voice: The Narrator in Paradise Lost*. Chicago: University of Chicago Press.

Fillmore, Charles. 1975. An Alternative to Checklist Theories of Meaning. In *Proceedings of the First Annual Meeting of the Berkeley Linguistics Society*, pp. 123-31. Berkeley: Berkeley Linguistics Society.

————. 1976. Topics in Lexical Semantics. In Peter Cole, ed., *Current Issues in Linguistic Theory*, pp. 76-138. Bloomington: Indiana University Press.

————. 1977. Scenes and Frames in Semantics. In Zampolli, pp. 55-81.

————. 1978. The Organization of Semantic Information in the Lexicon. In *Papers from the Parasession on the Lexicon*, pp. 1-11. Chicago: Chicago Linguistic Society.

————. 1982a. Towards a Descriptive Framework for Spatial Deixis. In R. J. Jarvella and W. Klein, eds., *Speech, Place, and Action*, pp. 31-59. London: John Wiley.

————. 1982b. Frame Semantics. In Linguistic Society of Korea, ed., *Linguistics in the Morning Calm,* pp. 111-38. Seoul: Hanshin.

————. 1985. Frames and the Semantics of Understanding. *Quaderni di Semantica* 6, no. 2, 222-54.

Finch, Henry Albert. 1957. An Explication of Counterfactuals by Probability Theory. *Philosophy and Phenomenological Research* 18:368-78.

Frye, Roland Mushat. 1960. *God, Man, and Satan*. Princeton, N.J.: Princeton University Press.

Gasking, Douglas. 1955. Causation and Recipes. *Mind* 64:479-87.

Gentner, Dedre. 1980. Metaphors and Models in Understanding Systems. Technical Report. Cambridge, Mass.: Bolt, Beranek, and Newman.

————. 1983. A Theoretical Framework for Analogy. *Cognitive Science* 7:155-70.

Gorovitz, Samuel. 1964. Leaving the Past Alone. *Philosophical Review* 73:360-71.

Gower, John. 1899. *Mirour de l'omme.* Ed. G. A. Macaulay. Oxford: Clarendon Press.

Hart, H. L. A., and A. M. Honoré. 1959. *Causation in the Law.* Oxford: Clarendon Press.

Henle, P. 1958. Metaphor. In *Language, Thought, and Culture.* Ann Arbor: University of Michigan Press.

Hjelmslev, Louis. 1961. *Prolegomena to a Theory of Language.* Trans. Frances J. Whitfield. Madison: University of Wisconsin Press.

Holland, Dorothy, and Naomi Quinn, eds. 1986. *Cultural Models in Language and Thought.* Cambridge: Cambridge University Press.

Hume, David. [1741] 1939. *An Inquiry Concerning Human Understanding.* In Edwin A. Burtt, ed., *The English Philosophers from Bacon to Mill.* New York: Modern Library.

Janda, Laura. 1984. A Semantic Analysis of the Russian Verbal Prefixes *ZA-, PERE-, DO-,* and *OT-.* Ph.D. diss., University of California, Los Angeles.

Johnson, Mark. 1987. *The Body in the Mind: The Bodily Basis of Reason and Imagination.* Chicago: University of Chicago Press.

Katz, J., and J. A. Fodor. 1963. The structure of a semantic theory. *Language* 39:170-210.

Kay, Paul. 1983. Linguistic Competence and Folk Theories of Language: Two English Hedges. In *Proceedings of the Ninth Annual Meeting of the Berkeley Linguistics Society,* pp. 128-37. Berkeley: Berkeley Linguistics Society. Reprinted in Holland and Quinn.

Kay, Paul, and Chad K. McDaniel. 1978. The Linguistic Significance of the Meanings of Basic Level Color Terms. *Language* 54:610-46.

Keenan, Edward L., ed. 1975. *Formal Semantics of Natural Language.* Cambridge: Cambridge University Press.

Kirk, G. S., and J. E. Raven. 1957. *The Presocratic Philosophers.* Cambridge: Cambridge University Press.

Lakoff, George. 1987. *Women, Fire, and Dangerous Things: What Categories Reveal About the Mind.* Chicago: University of Chicago Press.

Lakoff, George, and Mark Johnson. 1980. *Metaphors We Live By.* Chicago: University of Chicago Press.

Langacker, Ronald W. 1987. *Foundations of Cognitive Grammar.* Stanford: Stanford University Press.

Lanham, Richard A. 1968. *A Handlist of Rhetorical Terms: A Guide for Students of English Literature.* Berkeley: University of California Press.

Levin, Samuel. 1977. *The Semantics of Metaphor.* Baltimore: Johns Hopkins University Press.

Lévi-Strauss, Claude. 1969. *The Raw and the Cooked.* Trans. John Weightman and Doreen Weightman. New York: Harper and Row.

Lewis, David. 1973. *Counterfactuals.* Cambridge, Mass.: Harvard University Press.

Lindner, Susan. 1981. A Lexico-Semantic Analysis of Verb-Particle Constructions with *Up* and *Out.* Ph.D. diss., University of California, San Diego. Available from the Indiana University Linguistics Club.

————. 1982. What Goes Up Doesn't Necessarily Come Down: The Ins and Outs of Opposites. In *Proceedings of the Eighteenth Regional Meeting of the Chicago Linguistic Society,* pp. 305-23. Chicago: Chicago Linguistic Society.

Lucretius. 1975. *De Rerum Natura.* Trans. W. H. D. Rouse. Cambridge, Mass.: Harvard University Press.

McCall, Marsh H., Jr. 1969. *Ancient Rhetorical Theories of Simile and Comparison.* Cambridge, Mass.: Harvard University Press.

Mackie, J. L. 1962. Counterfactuals and Causal Laws. In R. J. Butler, ed., *Analytical Philosophy,* pp. 66-80. New York: Barnes and Noble.

————. 1974. *The Cement of the Universe.* Oxford: Clarendon Press.

————. 1975. Causes and Conditions. In Ernest Sosa, ed., *Causation and Conditionals,* pp. 15-38. Oxford: Oxford University Press.

McTaggart, John McTaggart Ellis. 1934. *Philosophical Studies.* London: E. Arnold.

Martianus Capella. 1925. *De Nuptiis Philologiae et Mercurii.* In Adolph Dick, ed., *Martianus Capella.* Leipzig: Teubner.

May, Herbert G., and Bruce M. Metzger. 1962. *The Oxford Annotated Bible.* Revised Standard Version. New York: Oxford University Press.

Metzing, Dieter, ed. 1980. *Frame Conceptions and Text Understanding.* New York: Walter de Gruyter.

Mill, John Stuart. 1843. *System of Logic.* London: John W. Parker.

Minsky, Marvin Lee, ed. 1968. *Semantic Information Processing.* Cambridge, Mass.: MIT Press.

Nagy, William. 1974. Figurative Patterns and Redundancy in the Lexicon. Ph.D. diss., University of California, San Diego.

O'Connor, D. J. 1951. The Analysis of Conditional Sentences. *Mind* 60:351-62.

Ortony, A., ed. 1979. *Metaphor and Thought*. Cambridge: Cambridge University Press.

Pears, D. F. 1956. The Priority of Causes. *Analysis* 17:54-63.

Peirce, Charles Sanders. 1931. *Collected Papers*. Ed. Charles Hartshorne and Paul Weiss. Cambridge, Mass.: Harvard University Press.

Philippson, Paula. 1936. *Genealogie als mythische Form: Studien zur Theogonie des Hesiod*. Oslo: A. W. Brøgger.

Popper, Karl R. 1949. A Note on Natural Laws and So-called "Contrary-to-fact Conditionals." *Mind* 58:62-66.

Pokorny, Julius. 1959. *Indogermanisches etymologisches Worterbuch*. Vol. 1. Bern: Francke Verlag.

Pritchard, James B., ed. 1955. *Ancient Near Eastern Texts Relating to the Old Testament*. 2d ed. Princeton, N.J.: Princeton University Press.

Putnam, Hilary. 1975. The Meaning of Meaning. In *Mind, Language, and Reality*. Cambridge: Cambridge University Press.

Reddy, Michael. 1979. The Conduit Metaphor. In Ortony, pp. 284-324.

Reid, Thomas. 1788. *Essays on the Active Powers of the Human Mind*. Essay 4.

Ricoeur Paul. 1974. Structure and Hermeneutics. In Don Ihde, ed., *The Conflict of Interpretations*. Evanston, Ill.: Northwestern University Press.

Rosch, Eleanor. 1977. Human Categorization. In N. Warren, ed., *Advances in Cross-Cultural Psychology*. New York: Academic Press.

Rosch, Eleanor, Carolyn Mervis, Wayne Gray, David Johnson, and Penny Boyes-Braem. 1976. Basic Objects in Natural Catagories. *Cognitive Psychology* 8:382-439.

Russell, Bertrand. 1917. On the Notion of Cause. In *Mysticism and Logic*. London: G. Allen and Unwin.

Schank, Roger. 1975. *Conceptual Information Processing*. Amsterdam: North-Holland.

Schneider, Erna F. 1952. Recent Discussion of Subjunctive Conditionals. *Review of Metaphysics* 6:623-47.

Schock, Rolf. 1961. Some Definitions of Subjunctive Implication, of Counterfactual Implication, and of Related Concepts. *Notre Dame Journal of Formal Logic* 2:206-21.

Searle, John. 1969. *Speech Acts*. London: Cambridge University Press.

———. 1975. A Taxonomy of Illocutionary Acts. In Keith Gunderson, ed., *Language, Mind, and Knowledge*. Minneapolis: University of Minnesota Press.

_____. 1983. *Intentionality: An Essay in the Philosophy of Mind.* Cambridge: Cambridge University Press.

Sellars, Wilfrid. 1958. Counterfactuals, Dispositions, and the Causal Modalities. In H. Feigel et al., eds., *Minnesota Studies in the Philosophy of Science,* 2:225-308. Minneapolis: University of Minnesota Press.

Sosa, Ernest. 1975. *Causation and Conditionals.* Oxford: Oxford University Press.

Stalnaker, Robert C., and Richard H Thomason. 1970. A Semantic Analysis of Conditional Logic. *Theoria* 36:23-42.

Steadman, John. 1959. *Milton's Epic Characters.* Chapel Hill: University of North Carolina Press.

Sweetser, Eve. In press. *Semantic Structure and Semantic Change.* Cambridge: Cambridge University Press.

Swinburne, R. G. 1966. Affecting the Past. *Philosophical Quarterly* 16:341-47.

Talmy, Leonard. 1972. Semantic Structures in English and Atsugewi. Ph.D. diss., University of California, Berkeley.

_____. 1975. Semantics and Syntax of Motion. In J. Kimball, ed., *Syntax and Semantics,* 4:181-238. New York: Academic Press.

_____. 1978. Relation of Grammar to Cognition. In D. Waltz, ed., *Proceedings of TINLAP-2 (Theoretical Issues in Natural Language Processing).* Champaign, Ill.: Coordinated Science Laboratory, University of Illinois.

_____. 1985. Force Dynamics in Language and Thought. In *Papers from the Parasession on Causatives and Agentivity.* Chicago: Chicago Linguistic Society.

Tversky, Barbara. 1985. Components and Categorization. In Craig, pp. 63-75.

Tversky, Barbara, and K. Hemenway. 1984. Objects, Parts, and Categories. *Journal of Experimental Psychology: General* 113:169-93.

Weber, Burton Jasper. 1971. *The Construction of Paradise Lost.* Carbondale: Southern Illinois University Press.

Wellek, René, and Austin Warren. 1949. *Theory of Literature.* New York: Harcourt, Brace, and World.

Wheelwright, P. 1962. *Metaphor and Reality.* Bloomington: Indiana University Press.

Wilks, Yorick. 1975a. Preference Semantics. In Edward L. Keenan, ed., *Formal Semantics of Natural Language,* pp. 329-35. Cambridge: Cambridge University Press.

_____. 1975b. A Preferential, Pattern-matching Semantics for Natural Language Understanding. *Artificial Intelligence* 6:53-74.

————. 1975c. Primitives and Words. In *Theoretical Issues in Natural Language Processing,* pp. 27-31. Cambridge, Mass: Bolt Beranek and Newman.

————. 1977. What Sort of Taxonomy of Causality Do We Need for Natural Language Understanding? *Cognitive Science* 2:235-64.

————. 1980. Frames, Semantics, and Novelty. In Metzing, pp. 134-63.

Wilson, John A. Egypt. In Henri Frankfort, ed., *Before Philosophy.* pp. 39-133. New York: Penguin, 1974.

Wittgenstein, Ludwig. 1958. *Philosophical Investigations.* 3d ed. Trans. G. E. M. Anscombe. New York: Macmillan.

Wright, Georg Henrik von. 1957. On Conditionals. In *Logical Studies,* pp. 127-65. London: Routledge and Kegan Paul.

————. 1971. *Explanation and Understanding.* Ithaca, N.Y.: Cornell University Press.

Zampolli, Antonio. 1977. *Linguistic Structures Processing.* Amsterdam: North-Holland.

Index

Index of Metaphors

General Index